JUST MAKE IT WORK

JUST MAKE IT WORK

AN HONEST GUIDE TO NAVIGATING THE FIRST DECADE OF YOUR CAREER

DONTÉ LEDBETTER

D. LEDBETTER

New York

ISBN-13: 978-0-578-76560-0 (Paperback)
Library of Congress Control Number: 2020919902

First edition January 2021.

D. Ledbetter

donteledbetter.com

To my family and friends, you all keep me grounded.

To my Dad, rest in peace.

"You may encounter many defeats, but you must not be defeated. In fact, it may be necessary to encounter the defeats, so you can know who you are, what you can rise from, how you can still come out of it."

- Maya Angelou

CONTENTS

PREFACE

Before the 2020 COVID-19 pandemic hit, I had just started a new job working for Yousician, a music learning platform based in Finland. I spent about five weeks between January 2020 and February 2020 in Helsinki, Finland, getting to know my fellow coworkers. After I returned from Europe, the COVID-19 pandemic overtook the United States. Lockdowns ensued, people got sick, people died, and millions lost their jobs almost instantly. Some people I know were either furloughed or laid off. I felt lucky that I was spared this fate, but I found myself wanting to help out.

I'm a very solutions-oriented person, which means when anyone comes to me with a problem, I try to solve it. I've become better at just letting others vent, but I can't help but try to fix things. I found myself sending job listings to friends who were laid off or just wanted to switch jobs. Then I got an epiphany about writing a book about careers. I never thought I could write a book. I've written a lot in my life, but a full-fledged book seemed out of reach. It turns out that I have more to say than I thought I did.

I've spent years mentoring and advising young professionals and college students on getting jobs and improving their careers. I find myself giving the same advice over and over again, which made me realize that many young professionals run into the same challenges within their first decade out of college or high school. Surprisingly, the millions of online articles that claim to give career advice don't seem to help these people much. As someone who is just now realizing that people admire and look up to me, I felt a duty to fill the void. Thus, this book was born.

INTRODUCTION: JUST MAKE IT WORK

I like to believe that one day I'll become a multi-millionaire and will never have to work a traditional job another day in my life. I've even considered buying lottery tickets and scratch-off games on a regular cadence to boost my chances (I didn't go through with it). The reality is I need to work, and I need something better than a 9–5 job. I have something they call a "career," which is just a fancy word for a series of 9–5 jobs with more fringe benefits than the crappy 9–5 jobs and longer work hours. Building a career that you're proud of isn't easy and straightforward. It's a marathon and can be annoying and frustrating, but it can also be rewarding when you finally find something that you're good at, have a desire to do, and get paid a lot of money to do.

When you're starting your career after college or high school, there's a lot you don't know about the "real world," but you have hope. You have hope for doing something that you love to do and maybe making a lot of money in the process. You have hope for avoiding the worst parts of the career-building process and getting your dream job quickly and with little effort. But your hope suddenly vanishes when you realize things aren't handed to you on a silver platter and that your plans don't align with the plans life has for you. But I'm here to bring the good news. There's a method for building a career you've always dreamed of. A career that you can look back on and be proud of. A career that has *you* written all over it.

Friends, peers, and other young professionals often ask me how I got to where I am professionally. I often don't have a straight answer. Now that I think of it, I've been lazy at giving answers. In fact, I do have a method that I still use to this day. But the method isn't a framework that can be distilled into a PDF or blog post. It's not a finite roadmap. It's a way of thinking, a way of being, a way of learning, a way of growing. Some will say it's a personality trait or intangible skill that can't be taught. It's ultimately a mindset and lifestyle.

The mindset of "just making it work," which is a mindset I live by, is a powerful mindset. It's one that's built upon will, grit, savviness, and an ounce of manipulation. "Just make it work" is also something you might hear as you go throughout your career. There are often moments when you just need to figure something out and pull a bunny out of your ass to get something done or hit a goal. I've heard similar phrases to "just make it work" while working for startups most of my career. Startups often don't have pristine processes for doing things or hitting goals. So, when a super aggressive goal needs to be hit, and the pressure is on, the hacking mentality takes over, and you just "figure it out" or "make it work."

This is a book about honesty. Honesty about what it takes to navigate the first decade of your career and reach your desired destination when life is unpredictable. Throughout the book, I'll share stories of my personal experiences and give you tips that you can apply to your own career. Everybody's path and career will look a little different, but there are common challenges that almost everyone needs to face (e.g., applying for a job). With this book, I hope to dispel some of the myths that are lingering out there on the interwebs. I also hope to give you inspiration for your approach to build a successful career because a career is something that needs to be actively managed and attacked.

However, by no means am I guaranteeing success. Life is unpredictable, and you may run into roadblocks even with the right tips, tools, and tactics. There's no surefire way to always get the job you want, the salary you want, or the opportunities you want. You can't control outcomes, but you can control your effort and approach. The only things that are certain in life are death, taxes, and getting an automated rejection email from the 20th company you've applied for.

CHAPTER 1: FALSE START

The thing I was never taught about starting anything meaningful is that the start doesn't actually matter. Where you end up is not determined by where you start—at least most of the time.

I grew up in a housing project in New York City. All I knew until I was eighteen years old was the sound of police sirens, gunshots, beer and urine in the stairwells, summer fights, roaches big and small, gangs, and nosy adults sitting outside my building waiting for the next bit of drama. Growing up in that environment, the future doesn't look too bright. In fact, you don't really think about the distant future. What happens tomorrow is the only thing that matters. Do I have enough money to eat tomorrow? Will I see my friends tomorrow? The future was a distant entity I was never able to fully understand until it came knocking on my door.

I never had any thoughts about going to college. Finishing high school was the ultimate goal. In my mind, college was only for wealthy or really gifted kids. Thanks to my high school college counselor, those assumptions were swiftly laid to rest. Once I learned about college loans, grants, and scholarships, my thoughts about my future changed dramatically, and I made it my goal to get to college by any means necessary, even if it meant getting into debt.

Like many seventeen-year-olds, I didn't exactly know what I wanted to do in life. My dream of making it to the National Basketball Association (NBA) was short-lived. Accounting? Sounds boring. Engineering? Sounds complicated. So, when it came time to choose a college major, I chose to study what I loved and had a passion for: sports. I majored in Sport and Recreation Management at Temple University in Philadelphia, which has one of the top sports management programs in the United States. I wanted to make up for my failed NBA dream by possibly infiltrating the league through other professional avenues. Sports was what I knew inside and out. I was a kid who lived and breathed sports, so it only made sense to spend my student loan and scholarship money to pursue a career in sports.

I studied at Temple University for two years until I decided to transfer out to prevent going into an obscene amount of student loan debt. I came back to New York and studied for an additional two years at State University of New York (SUNY) at New Paltz in New Paltz, New York. Since SUNY New Paltz didn't have a sports management program, I was forced to choose the next best thing. I had a little experience with social media marketing during my time as a student marketing coordinator at a student association at Temple, so I chose to major in marketing. Little did I know, that would be one of the best decisions I've ever made in my life.

In hindsight, I certainly didn't think that a marketing degree would provide more career opportunities than a sports management degree, but that's exactly what happened. The decision to abandon my original dream of working in sports in favor of becoming a marketer wasn't a decision I wanted to make. I felt indecisive and not confident that a marketing career was something I was cut out for. But that early fork in the road—a true false start—was a blessing in disguise, and it all has to do with opportunity sizing.

Choosing a career path is always a tough decision, and many students and young professionals switch paths frequently early in their careers. When thinking about possible career paths to take, you should start by thinking in two ways: opportunity breadth and earning potential. Opportunity breadth is the number of opportunities that any given career path can yield in the future. Earning potential is the potential financial gains you may be able to achieve from a given career path.

Opportunity breadth helps you cast a wide net as you grow in your career. Thinking about opportunity breadth helps you avoid being pigeon-holed into one industry or one specific type of role. In my case, earning a marketing degree brought me more opportunity breadth and earning potential than earning a sports management degree would have. Because sports management is such a specific discipline for a specific industry, the opportunities to branch out from there are limited. Of course, I could've always made a pivot early in my career, but having a degree in sports management makes a pivot so much harder, especially if certain skills aren't transferable.

On the other hand, marketing is needed everywhere. Virtually every organization on the planet that wants people to care about what they do will need some sort of marketing. Even sports organizations need marketers, which made me realize that a sports management degree wasn't necessary. As a marketer, I have an endless number of places to work and opportunities to grow. As a college junior, it didn't hit me that I had just switched to a discipline that would unlock many doors for me years down the line. The decision to switch from a sports career path to a marketing career path is one that I don't regret.

Then there's earning potential. I'll preface my advice by saying that money is not the most important thing in life, and not every decision you make in your career should be driven by money. However, you need money. In some places, you need a lot of it to live and thrive. Unfortunately, not every career path or job will help you earn enough to live comfortably, and you'll need to make some hard decisions, which brings me to a really honest and somewhat controversial tip that I want to give you.

If you want to become a high earner, don't follow your passion. If your passion involves STEM (Science, Technology, Engineering, Math) or finance, then ignore my advice. But for the vast majority of you, your passion is probably something in the realm of an artistic pursuit, reading and writing, teaching, or some other interest that doesn't yield a lot in salary in the job world (of course, there are exceptions). For me, that passion is photography. I would love to get paid to do photography, but the reality is photography wouldn't generate nearly enough income to match what I make now as a marketer in tech. Very few companies hire full-time photographers, and most photographers work on a freelance basis. Unfortunately, for my financial plans, freelance photography is too unpredictable, and I hate obnoxious and indecisive clients.

This is not to say that you shouldn't become a teacher, police officer, or any other professional that's considered essential to society. Our kids need more good teachers who can make a difference, and our society needs better police officers who treat everyone fairly. But realize that when you walk down those career paths, the biggest benefit doesn't come in the form of a salary. Changing lives and protecting society is enough of a benefit to make those career paths worth the discounted salary. In the 21st century, the career paths that would get you anywhere close to becoming a high earner early in your career are STEM-related and business-related (e.g., marketing or sales). There are obviously a few exceptions, but your chances of making six figures in the first decade of your career are higher if you focus on those two areas.

My story is one of the millions of false-start stories. I've met many people whose careers look nothing like their beginnings. That's because your beginning doesn't mean anything. This applies to your career choices as well as any predicament you were in early in your life. Yes, there are mountains of data that suggest that when people are born into poverty (like I was), they have a good chance of never being able to claw out of it. And yes, there are many people who go on to fulfill their original dreams without ever changing course or pivoting. However, it all doesn't matter because life gives you chances to get on the right track, even when the ride is a bit bumpy in the beginning.

I'm one of those people who loves the idea of having nine lives (wouldn't it be awesome if we can get nine do-overs in life?). Unfortunately, we all have one life and die once at the end of it. But during your life, you get opportunities. Opportunities to change your mind, rewind, be successful, screw up and make mistakes, and do it all again multiple times. That's probably the best thing about life. One decision, one start doesn't have to define you.

There will be many opportunities to pivot and make changes throughout your career. Some of the most successful people we know started in unexpected places. For example, J. K. Rowling was a waitress before she became a multi-millionaire author. My pivot came during college, and I have never looked back since. Your pivot may be five years into your career when you realize that you hate your $400,000 job bumping heads with Wall Street scumbags, and in fact, you would rather be teaching third graders for one-tenth of that amount or fighting climate change for a cash-strapped non-profit.

At the end of the day, what matters is how you navigate the journey, how you capitalize on opportunities that come your way, and how you hunt for the opportunities that seem too hard to grasp.

CHAPTER 2: THE HUNT

The excitement washed over me as I secured my first post-college phone interview with a cool, big-name company based in Massachusetts: TripAdvisor. I don't quite remember the role I applied for, but I certainly remember the interview process.

You see, there wasn't actually much of an interview process. I had my first phone interview scheduled for a Monday with one of TripAdvisor's recruiters. Monday came, and I received no call from the recruiter at the scheduled time. "Things happen," I thought to myself, and I proceeded to follow up with the recruiter via email. She sent me an apology, and we rescheduled the phone interview for that Wednesday. Wednesday came, and once again, I received no call from the recruiter. Now, I'm not one who enjoys confrontation, but to me, this circumstance warranted a "let-me-speak-to-your-manager" moment. As a college grad with no job lined up after graduation, I was in no mood to waste time or have my time be wasted by a recruiter who couldn't afford me the luxury of a simple call.

I used whatever savvy internet-stalking skills I had to find the email address of the head of recruiting at TripAdvisor at the time. I sent the guy a long email detailing how I had scheduled two phone interviews with his recruiter without a callback and vehemently expressed how unprofessional the whole process was. As a side note, I was super proud of myself and how I handled the situation. There's a level of assertiveness that I showed in that situation that came in handy time and time again in my career. TripAdvisor's head of recruiting shockingly replied to my email and invited me to a phone call.

During the phone call, he expressed his apologies and explained the situation behind the abandoned phone calls. I don't remember the full conversation, but there's one thing that he said that opened the black box on the whole recruiting process. According to TripAdvisor's head of recruiting, there were multiple people already being considered for the role internally, and the external job posting wasn't supposed to be live, and the mean recruiter lady wasn't supposed to be interviewing anyone externally.

The feeling of enlightenment was stronger than my feeling of disbelief. Yes, it was disappointing that I actually had no chance of getting this job, and the recruiter had toyed with my time and emotions. But it was somewhat intriguing to know that the competition for any given job opening doesn't just include other anxious job seekers outside the company; it also includes the hungry employees within the company. This is a phenomenon that I didn't think anyone else my age knew, and after my conversation with TripAdvisor's head of recruiting, I was hell-bent on circumventing it.

Looking for a professional full-time job for the very first time is daunting. If you're not one of the lucky new grads who has a paid internship, trainee program spot, or full-time job already lined up, you're in for an emotional battle when looking for your first job. I'm naturally a perfectionist (to a fault), so I fully expected to graduate into a full-time job. That was the one thing I was striving for throughout college, which is why I did a total of three internships, spent countless hours perfecting my résumé, and even gave up going to some college parties because I had to wake up the next morning and attend a networking event. The hard work had to pay off and culminate in a full-time job straight out of college. But life had its way, and I found myself back home without any means of income and no way of helping my mother pay rent.

I can count on one hand how many times I've been depressed in my life. I'm not someone who gets down about many things. Not meeting my own expectations of having a job out of college was one of the times I've been depressed. That depression manifested itself in my lack of desire to leave my house and communicate with friends. I felt like a failure for not having a job. There were even days when I skipped taking a shower because of a lack of desire to do anything but sit on my couch and apply for jobs. Days turned into nights, but I didn't even notice because I didn't turn the light on or off in my living room. Every hour felt the same.

Eventually, my luck changed, and I received interview invitations from several companies. One company wanted to hire me as a paid intern, which I thought was below me. I had an in-person interview with the Oxford University Press on Fifth Avenue in New York City. The office was darker than I thought it would be, but the thought of working for an organization with a reputable name intrigued me. Then, I was invited to interview with an advertising technology startup in New York City's SoHo neighborhood. This scrappy, five-person startup wasn't the corporate job I was hoping for, but they were willing to pay me as a full-time employee, the CEO was down to earth, SoHo was a cool neighborhood, and the co-working space was electric. With a swift decision, I accepted the role as a marketing coordinator and began my journey in New York City's tech scene.

After being unemployed for a mere two months, which felt like two years, I finally had a job. But there's a lot that I did up until that point that I want to share. The first piece that helped me throughout my job hunt was my resilience. In spite of my mild depression, I was able to stay focused on my goal of getting a job, even if that meant sacrificing social interaction.

When things don't go as well as you expect, it's easy to lose hope and lose steam, and the job hunt will always be a situation that's unpredictable. Your expectations will almost never be quite met. They'll either be surpassed or not come close to being met. If the latter happens, depression and other negative feelings typically follow. As a job hunter, you have to be prepared for this and build up the capacity to rebound from any setbacks. Be prepared for things to not move as fast as you would like them to. Be prepared to power through job applications and constant résumé and cover letter revisions. And be prepared for rejections, which brings me to my next point.

Rejection sucks. In dating, in job hunting, in all aspects of life, being rejected doesn't feel good. Why is it so horrible for our egos? Because it feels like an indictment on us. We feel personally attacked and devalued when we get rejected. I'm not a psychologist, but I can imagine adopted children feel the same way about not feeling wanted by their biological parents. Someone rejecting you is basically them saying "I don't want you." Hearing that puts a dagger into your heart, and if you're not careful, it demoralizes you for a long time.

Rejection is a way of life in the job hunt. You're not perfect, so there's very little chance you'll get a job offer for every job you apply for. Add that to the fact that there's a mountain of competition for any one job (including internal competition). When applying for my first job, my heart would always pound faster every time I received an email from an employer. And my heart would drop every time the opening sentence of the email read like a rejection email.

How do you get around rejection to get the job you want? It's easier said than done, but the very first thing is accepting that rejection is normal. Rejections are like red lights on a road trip. You don't complain about them, you just get through them on your way to your ultimate destination. It's often said that you need to experience something over and over again to become immune to it. The more you're rejected, the less it should affect you. Getting rejected for the first time feels like the end of the world. But your tenth rejection becomes an expectation because you know it's a necessary evil.

Rejection can also be turned into something that you should always crave: feedback. Every recruiter or hiring manager has a reason or two for hiring someone over you or just rejecting you outright. Turn this into an opportunity to ask why you were rejected. To warn you, not everyone will want to give you feedback. In fact, some companies will send you automated rejection emails that explicitly say, "We cannot give you feedback." But luckily, there are pleasant recruiters out there who are more than willing to give you constructive feedback. Embrace it.

The third point is grittiness and how that can be translated into tactics. The job-hunting process isn't very transparent. The methods and processes that recruiting teams and hiring managers use to filter out candidates are obviously not publicly available. And the recruiting systems created by companies such as ADP and Greenhouse are meant to make life easier for recruiting teams, not you. This means that there's a lot you don't know about the process, and sending off your résumé is basically like throwing darts while blindfolded. To give yourself the best chance of being seen and heard by recruiters, you have to resort to grittiness.

One piece of advice I give to every job seeker is to always reach out to hiring managers and recruiters, in addition to uploading your résumé to the online portal. This doesn't always work, and sometimes it can be hard to find the email addresses of certain people. But it gives you an opportunity to make the case for yourself in a more direct channel and shows that you know how to take initiative. You would be surprised how many candidates still don't reach out via email. Cold email is not nearly as scary as cold calling. All it takes is a few minutes of typing. The responses you'll get from a cold email will vary. Some recruiters and hiring managers won't respond, some will just direct you to the application site, and some will schedule a call with you immediately.

I once cold emailed a recruiter at Nike regarding a role that I knew I wasn't qualified for. Nike is one of my favorite companies that I would love to work for. This cold email was an experiment to see if I would get a response. A day after sending my email, not only did I receive a response but I also had a 30-minute conversation with a recruiter. We agreed that I wasn't qualified for the role, but there were many other roles at their Oregon headquarters that I should explore in the future. Cold email responses aren't guaranteed, but giving yourself a better shot is always needed, and that's all that matters when job hunting. Job hunting is a numbers and opportunity game. You want more opportunities to be seen and heard.

You can take the grittiness a step further and really go above and beyond. I'm all for being as efficient as possible when it comes to job hunting, which means not doing anything that requires an extraordinary amount of time. But I also believe in putting effort into something that you really want. There are examples of candidates who go above and beyond by doing things like mailing letters to potential employers, creating solutions to an actual business problem of employers, and doing all sorts of viral tactics just to get the attention of the employer.

I've never gone to those extremes, but I leaned into my cold emailing skills by writing subject lines like "Looking for your next marketing coordinator?" and "Want a better chance at hitting your marketing goals?" Clearly, I approached things like a salesperson, but I felt I needed to be scrappy (and a little annoying) like a salesperson. To me, getting a job was just a matter of brute force, and I had to send as many of these emails alongside my résumé as much as possible. To this day, this tactic still works in my favor.

The fourth point is a point of choice and opportunity. There may be thousands of open roles in your field or discipline that you could potentially apply for. Which ones do you go after? It's simply a matter of preference and personal goals. Do you want to work for a big company or a smaller company? You'll have more impact at a startup, but you'll have more potential to grow at an established corporation.

What industry do you want to work in? Healthcare, e-commerce, finance, education? There are tons more. What types of problems do you want to solve? Think along a spectrum. Tobacco company or fight for climate change? (Tobacco doesn't really solve problems). Decisions, decisions. What types of customers do you want to serve? B2B (business-to-business; think IBM) or B2C (business-to-consumer; think McDonald's)?

These are questions you should answer before you go on the job hunt. But admittedly, as a new grad, sometimes you won't have a clear idea of what you want. That's okay. Your first job is a learning experience, and it doesn't have to be the perfect role.

As a marketing major, I read about and admired the father of advertising, David Ogilvy. I had aspirations of being a copywriter for an agency and working on cool advertising campaigns for brands like Nike and Coca-

Cola. My first job didn't satisfy that aspiration at all. I was hired to do content marketing for a small ad-tech startup and help drive website traffic and leads through blog posts, social media, e-books, and digital ads. Our customers were other businesses and small advertisers, not the millions of consumers that I dreamed about. This was not a job that I dreamed about one bit, but the learning experience was great, and as you will read in the next few chapters, I got a lot out of it.

Lastly, consider the reality that your first full-time job will likely be an entry-level role. An entry-level role is designed to provide candidates with a stepping-stone into the company. It's also designed to help employers off-load remedial tasks. That's the honest truth. The entry-level role has suffered in recent years as more companies search for candidates with at least some experience who can make an immediate impact. This is why most "entry-level" roles will require a few years of experience. And those remedial tasks that entry-level hires have done in the past are now being automated or outsourced to inexpensive freelancers.

As someone who may not have years of experience, this gives you a serious disadvantage and makes your job search much harder. The counterpunch to this handicap is your skill set. It's no secret that hard skills (e.g., Excel, coding) are what's most important for an entry-level role. Soft skills become more important over time. What employers look for is whether or not your résumé aligns with the role and your base skill set can be applied to the role, even if your years of experience fall short. Years of experience is not a strict condition most of the time, and employers will make an exception for candidates with the right attitude who have shown an effort to improve their skills. Let your skills shine on your résumé. It's one of the only effective weapons you have as someone who doesn't have deep experience.

Securing your first job will feel like your biggest accomplishment. You braved the job hunt and may or may not have gotten the job you wanted, but you certainly got the job you needed. You're now a full-time employee of some promising company or Fortune 500 conglomerate. Congratulations, you're just getting started.

CHAPTER 3: THE SIX-MONTH RULE

Having a real job is a big freaking deal. Taxes have to be paid, decisions have to be made about 401(k)s and health plan options, and you actually have to take something seriously for the very first time in your life because the repercussions could possibly mean being homeless (yay adult life). Your first full-time job out of school will most likely be nothing like what you imagined. The expectations for a new hire vary widely depending on the role and experience level. Your manager should make it clear what the expectations are, and if that doesn't happen, it's up to you to seek clarity so everyone has an understanding. However, regardless of the expectation, you should have one goal as a new hire and that's to make the greatest impact that you possibly can in your first six months.

On a timescale of months, years, and decades, six months is not a lot of time. But six months is enough time to prove yourself to your new employer. In fact, it's the only chance you have to prove yourself to your new employer before your new-hire aura starts to evaporate. Why is this the case? For one, managers need to be proven right. Every hiring manager takes a risk when hiring someone new. You never know if a new hire will end up being who they say they are in the long run.

As a new hire, it's your job to validate the hiring decision of your manager. That needs to happen in the first six months. Six months is two business quarters, and your leash gets really short if you've made no meaningful contributions six months into your role. But I don't recommend just doing what you're supposed to do; I recommend going above and beyond. I recommend being the best employee they've ever hired.

My first job out of college was a bit overwhelming. I was the only marketing hire at the company, and I was responsible for everything related to marketing, including social media, design, digital advertising, blogging, website optimization, and even event planning. That's a lot for a new buck out of college to handle, but I made it a priority to show my manager (who was the CEO) that I was capable of handling any challenge. Furthermore, I simply wanted to impress everyone.

I've always believed that first impressions mean everything in all aspects of life. I wanted to hit a home run as soon as I landed the role, no matter how challenging. Within my first six months, I hit that home run, and I hit it deep. Our weekly site traffic increased by over 200 percent, and sign ups increased by over 100 percent thanks to my blogging and social media efforts. I was also miraculously able to take a very small budget—about $700 a week—and drive $130,000 in revenue in one quarter just from social media ads. Not only did my ego explode, but I was also viewed as an all-star at the company. I had the machismo of a ten-year veteran, and I had just graduated a few months prior.

A little over a year and a half later, I found myself in the same situation at a different company. After 20 months at my first company, I re-entered the job market and found a role at a promising marketing technology startup in the Garment District in New York City, a few blocks away from Times Square. This was my first time making a job transition. I understood that your résumé will only get you into the door. Once you're there, no one will be impressed by your résumé. You have to deliver, and I did exactly that.

As a content marketer, my job was to create compelling content for other marketers, to drive leads for the sales team. Weeks into my new role at my second company, I spent hours every day and night trying to think of a content idea that our customers and prospects would swoon over. That's easier said than done as there's a heap of online content about all sorts of different topics. During my research, I came up with an idea that was super simple yet hadn't been created before.

The practice of mobile marketing skyrocketed after the introduction of the iPhone in 2007. New roles and departments were created, millionaires were minted, new companies were founded to help companies excel at mobile marketing, and online content about mobile marketing proliferated the internet. While researching content ideas during my first month at my second company, I realized that there was no single source of truth for frequently asked questions (FAQs) related to mobile marketing. Somehow, all these influencers and press sites glossed over something so simple. No one could explain mobile marketing and its various components in layman's terms. So, I came up with the not-so-genius idea of creating an e-book highlighting the top 50 mobile marketing FAQs.

The idea was eventually green-lighted by my manager, and I wrote a 50-page e-book in two weeks. Once it launched, the e-book managed to drive 30 percent of all the company's website leads in its first month. Over its lifespan, it received multiple links and mentions from various industry experts, company blogs, and it has been downloaded by marketers from all over the world. Uber, Amazon, Airbnb, Alibaba, and The New York Times are just a few big-name companies whose marketers downloaded the e-book. My creation and early success were well-received, and it eventually set the tone for the rest of my time at the company. The successful e-book that I created for my second company was game-changing in a variety of ways, but its impact made significant progress toward my number goal at the time: leads.

What does it mean to "win" at a job? "Winning" and doing well at a job is a matter of progress and perception. Almost every performance-driven company on the planet sets goals, whether quantitative or qualitative. Your impact as an employee is judged by your ability to make progress toward those goals. Why is making progress toward a goal more important than actually hitting a goal? Progress puts your work and effort front and center. It's easy for people to gauge impact when they see a number increase, the lines on a graph get higher, or the needle on a dial move in the right direction. Progress validates your work, and it's important to show people that you're making progress.

It's also important for executives to know that their teams are making progress. Now, I'm not advocating for never having the drive to hit a goal. Hitting goals are important for a variety of business-related reasons. However, some companies are bad at setting attainable goals, some companies set stretch goals that aren't meant to actually be hit with a reasonable amount of work and effort, and most meaningful company goals require the efforts of multiple teams, not just individual contribution.

Your progress also has to be obvious. You have to find a way to make your achievements known in a non-egotistical way. This is when your internal public relations (PR) come into play. Your internal PR matters to your reputation. Good internal PR will put you in a category of employees who are desired, needed, and somewhat indispensable. These are the company's all-stars. These are employees that a company wouldn't want to let go of in the worst circumstances because they're just that good.

Then there's bad and neutral PR. Most employees will fit into the neutral PR category (bad PR employees are the ones who get fired). They come to work, do their jobs, and go home. They don't want attention and recognition. Or maybe they want it but don't know how to get it. These employees, for the most part, will do their jobs well. However, it may be a little harder for these people to get raises and promotions and to be invited to work on new and exciting projects for the company.

When chasing upward mobility in a company, the best way to give yourself a fighting chance is to improve your reputation for making an impact, and not just among the nucleus of your manager and close teammates. It's expected that your manager and close coworkers will know about your achievements, but the broader company will most likely have no clue about how and what you've contributed. This isn't a bad thing in itself, but to rise in the ranks faster, your work needs to be known around the company. People need to know who you are, and not because you're the loudest, most fashionable, or funniest person in the company. They need to know you because you get things done.

In a business environment, there's generally a right and wrong way to advocate for yourself and make your progress known. We all hate those people who like to brag and take credit for everything. Those people are self-centered, ego-centric, and not seen as team players. You don't want to be that person under any circumstances. In this day and age, collaboration and teamwork are seen as the gold standard of working to achieve business goals. Your personal achievements are second to any achievement of the team, and gloating about your personal achievements puts a bad taste in your coworkers' mouths. The more non-asshole way to make your work known is through strategic advocating and perception.

The phrase "out of sight, out of mind" is important when working to build your internal PR. There will always be a perception that the employees and teams who aren't heard from are the ones not contributing, even if it's far from the truth. The only exception to this rule is engineers, who are known for being more introverted and quieter. For a non-engineer, there has to be a perception that there's progress being made, and ideally, that perception is rooted in reality. A good way to foster this perception is to stick to transparent progress updates.

Nowadays, most companies try to create an environment where progress toward goals and progress on key initiatives and campaigns can be shared via email or a chat platform like Slack. These processes are primarily put in place to foster transparency and communication, which is essential to any business. These updates are your primary channel for showing what you and the team has done. Most of these types of updates are sent by department heads or team leads, so if you're not either of those people, you most likely won't have direct access to post any progress or updates in those channels.

If this is the case, you must advocate for yourself and your team to your manager, team lead, or department head. Become the best lobbyist there is, and make sure that the work of your team—not just yours—is known. This kills two birds with one stone. Not only are you advocating for yourself, but you're lifting up those around you. You become a self-confident team player.

There will also be other avenues and opportunities to boost your internal PR. For example, many companies have demo days, where employees throughout the company can demonstrate what they're working on. This is prime time for you. If you're not someone who gets the spotlight often, this is an opportunity you can't shy away from. Learn to become an advocate for yourself and your team by participating in public forums and discussions in your company. Participation doesn't win you an award, but it gets you noticed, and that's what matters. If you're someone who fears public speaking, make it a priority to rid yourself of the fear. It'll only benefit you in the long run.

Now, all this is easier said than done, and if you're taking on a role at a large corporation, this strategy can be challenging to execute. A sea of 100,000 employees will not likely know or care about what impact you've made. But even at a larger firm, this strategy can apply to your direct team or department. And if you're someone who works at a smaller company, say, a 100-person start-up, this strategy can work wonders for you.

Ultimately, you don't have to be popular to be known; you just have to be present. In your first six months, you have to master progress and perception. Don't shy away from the spotlight. Constantly figure out subtle ways to get the results of your work into the open, but don't push or act in desperation.

The moments will come. You just have to wait for them like a lion hunting gazelle.

CHAPTER 4: WATCH OUT, IMPOSTER

A year after joining my first company, I was deeply observant of everything that was going on in our industry. We were in advertising technology, and the industry was booming with new companies and new competitors. There was also a trend of smaller ad-tech firms being acquired by bigger ad-tech firms. As in every industry, when new players enter, some larger market leaders feel threatened. One of the best, monopolistic ways to squash your competition is to acquire them (just ask Facebook). This was all exciting to me. As a relatively new grad, I was unfamiliar with this type of market dynamics and fast-paced innovation. It seemed as if my business courses in college completely skipped over these details.

I found myself in a unique position to write something about what I was seeing in the industry. Not only was I regularly blogging and had a following through my company's blog, but our company's name was also starting to make a little noise in the New York ad-tech scene. We were small, but more and more people caught a whiff of who we were, thanks to some press that featured our co-founders and my content marketing prowess. I felt that it was my obligation to write something regarding acquisitions in ad-tech, and that's what I did.

While writing the blog post, I realized that there weren't any press articles covering this acquisition bonanza in ad-tech. After all, it was pretty obvious what was happening. It seemed that no one cared to write about ad-tech acquisitions. I saw this as an opportunity to elevate my argument and pitch my piece to the press.

Now, I'll just flat out say my cold emailing skills around this time sucked. I was a 23-year-old with one year of professional experience under my belt, and I knew nothing about what type of guest articles press websites wanted. But I didn't care. I thought my argument was good enough to be read by sophisticated readers. I reached out to a journalist at a website called VentureBeat, which is a news site that covers trends in the tech industry. Reaching out to journalists and press is always hit-or-miss. Most journalists have built a filter for bullshit news stories and have a high standard for what they cover. I never expected my piece on ad-tech acquisitions to get picked up. It seemed too good to be true. However, to my surprise, VentureBeat was interested in publishing my piece in the contributor section of their website.

There I was, a 23-year-old with a year's worth of experience, about to have a contributor piece on one of the most reputable tech news sites around. I felt confident. It was a sign that my thoughts were validated, and people cared about what I had to say. The day it was published, I was filled with excitement. I posted it almost anywhere I possibly could on social media through my personal accounts and company accounts. The likes, shares, and retweets came in, and I was drunk off of dopamine. It was going well. Almost too well. Readers of VentureBeat started to comment on the piece. Almost all the comments were analytical and positive. However, there was one comment that hit me deep in the gut.

I don't remember his name, his job title, or his comment verbatim. But I do remember the sentiment of his comment. One of the commenters of my guest piece made it a point to highlight my credentials, implying that I was too junior to have an opinion on the topic of adtech acquisitions. His comment was something along the lines of "Why are we reading this from a junior-level marketer?" He didn't even state whether or not he agreed with what I wrote. His only priority was pointing out my age and experience, something that wasn't obvious in the article itself. My experience could've only been known through my LinkedIn profile, which I assume he visited. My feelings weren't hurt by any means, but my confidence took a hit. I was knocked off my cloud, my high was ended, and that was my first time experiencing imposter syndrome.

The feeling of imposter syndrome is one of the worst feelings you can feel in the workplace. Not only do you feel inadequate and undeserving, even despite all your success, but you also lose a little motivation. The motivation that you rode on your way to your success is now in limbo. Doubts cloud your decision-making, and it all makes you shy away from the spotlight, in fear of criticism. You'll be less likely to advocate for yourself, which can hurt your long-term prospects of getting the recognition you deserve. Furthermore, studies show that imposter syndrome can lead to depression and anxiety.[1] Luckily, there are ways to defeat imposter syndrome and get your mojo back.

First, it's important to understand that there are different ways imposter syndrome can manifest itself. In my case, my imposter syndrome was triggered by an external critique. Before that comment, my confidence was at an all-time high. The comment brought me down to earth and then some. In my opinion, this type of imposter syndrome is easier to eradicate. As a young professional, I wasn't used to a ton of criticism from people outside of teachers and girlfriends. Getting criticism from a stranger in the industry was a reality check for me. It made me realize that nothing I do will satisfy everyone, and there will always be naysayers, devil's advocates, and true haters. This is something I had to build up a tolerance for, and I think you should do the same.

Understand that criticism and disagreement is normal, especially if you're doing anything important that is worth doing. Furthermore, some people will prejudge you based on what they think they know about you. They'll use your background, experience, or any other so-called weapon to bring you down. Your best defense is tolerance. Tolerance and a dose of indifference.

Once you learn to expect unreasonable dissent, you'll get used to receiving it. That doesn't mean it won't hurt every time you get it. It'll hurt like hell to get criticized by assholes who just want to hurt you and put you down. But it won't be detrimental. It won't knock you down or make you question yourself. The only exception to this method is constructive feedback and dissent. Learn to learn from disagreements and contrary arguments. Being open-minded is one of the best traits that you can exhibit in the workplace.

But imposter syndrome is not only something that's influenced by external forces. In fact, most of the cases of imposter syndrome start within. That means it's something that your mind forces upon you. In her book *The Secret Thoughts of Successful Women: Why Capable People Suffer From the Imposter Syndrome and How to Thrive in Spite of It*, Dr. Valerie Young categorizes imposter syndrome into five subgroups: the Perfectionist, the Superwoman/man, the Natural Genius, the Soloist, and the Expert.[2]

The Perfectionist group, which I consider myself a part of, consists of people who have extremely high standards and exhibit control freak tendencies. Failure is not an option for these people and every project has to be 100 percent perfect. When it's not, these people are not satisfied and often have self-doubt. To circumvent this type of imposter syndrome, understand that failure is a part of any process and perfection is something that can't actually be achieved.

This is admittedly easier said than done and requires self-discipline and retraining your brain to embrace failure and the concept of progress. Failure and mistakes will always happen. You have to train your mind to accept this and redefine what it means to "fail." Failure is not losing. Failure is not being inadequate. Failure is learning. Failure doesn't mark an ending. Failure is a part of natural growth and learning.

The second group Dr. Young mentions is called the "Superwoman/man." People in this group need validation from others to feel worthy. They over-work just so they can measure up to others, and they let the opinions of others dictate their self-confidence. This is an easy group to fall into, especially early on in your career. As someone who's young and new, you feel that you need to work harder than everyone else so people will accept you. Maybe there's a coworker that everyone admires, and you don't want to be seen as less competent than that person. Being in this group has the potential to damage you mentally and physically.

How does the six-month rule mentioned in the last chapter relate to the Superwoman/man group that Dr. Young mentions? The key difference is that when practicing the six-month rule, you're not seeking validation to feel good about your work nor are you trying to measure up to anyone else. You're simply increasing the visibility of your progress and successes. In other words, it's not about the feeling you get from the perception others have of you; it's about creating a narrative for yourself and establishing your personal brand, so others in the company will know who you are, what you're about, and how you can make an impact.

It's important not to confuse the two. The six-month rule is your personal brand and PR strategy. Being in Dr. Young's Superwoman/man group means being reliant on external validation and driven by the approval of others, which leads to imposter syndrome.

The third group Dr. Young mentions is called the "Natural Genius." These are people who seem to succeed without much effort. They're known for being the smartest in the room and always have solutions to problems when no one else does. This group is similar to the Perfectionists in that they have high expectations for themselves. But they differ in that the people in the "Natural Genius" group don't like to be taught, mentored, managed, or coached. This group can benefit from practicing more humility. Try engaging in something you're not good at and embrace the process of learning. You won't know everything, and that's okay.

The fourth group Dr. Young mentions is called the "Soloist." People in the "Soloist" group don't like asking for help. They're people who feel weak when they ask for help and believe they need to accomplish things on their own. The "Soloist" is related to the "Natural Genius" in that they may feel like their genius-status is threatened by external help. There's a perception that geniuses don't ask for help. They just know how to figure things out. Both of these imposter syndrome types force you to create silos around yourself. To get around this, learn to value help and separate weakness from help. Do some soul-searching to figure out what you're not so good at or what you could use guidance on. Know your weaknesses (there will always be weaknesses).

The last group Dr. Young mentions is called the "Expert." People in this group have an insatiable appetite for more information—to a fault. They feel the need to know everything about a specific area. And if they don't know everything, they feel inadequate, inexperienced, and ill-equipped. To get around this, first, realize that you won't know everything there is to know about any given topic. Think about it; experienced biologists are constantly learning new things about the human body. Being an expert doesn't mean knowing everything there is to know. In fact, it's virtually impossible to know everything about complex topics. Stick to learning the information you need to know to excel at your job and be willing to learn more when you need to, but no more than you have to.

I've admittedly fallen into all five of these imposter groups at multiple points in my career, and I know what it feels like to let these archetypes get the best of you. Your productivity can suffer, and most importantly, your mental health can suffer. Completely eradicating imposter syndrome is a career-long battle. It will continue to crop up just like the weeds in a yard.

Your best weapon is your ability to be vulnerable and embrace learning, failure, criticism, and humility. Only then will you be able to keep those annoying weeds out of your yard.

CHAPTER 5: HACKING YOUR GROWTH

It's become somewhat of a hobby of mine to look at the career paths of Fortune 500 corporate executives on LinkedIn. You might be wondering if I have better things to do with my life, and I promise I do, but there's something so fascinating about this group of people. Why am I so fascinated by this group specifically?

A lot of these folks have done something that seems almost impossible for my generation (millennials) to do: they've spent a decade or more at one company. Some have spent two or three decades at the same company! They've experienced almost every major life event while on the payroll of the same corporate conglomerate. I can't imagine spending five years in the same apartment let alone twenty years at the same company. What makes this group interesting is their growth stories. What types of roles did they have in their careers? What enabled them to grow? What type of company guidelines around advancement did they have to follow? These are all questions that you will eventually be able to answer in thirty years. But first thing's first, how do you craft your own growth plan and "hack" your growth to achieve career advancement?

Let's start with the *why*. Why do you need a growth plan? If you're someone who hopes to have a leadership or managerial role, have a more prominent job title, or make more money, you need a growth plan. Achieving more than what you currently have requires strategic thinking and a roadmap of how to get to where you want to go. Without a strategy or a roadmap for career advancement, you'll find yourself stuck and left behind.

You may find yourself never making more or doing more than what you're currently doing because you lacked a forward-thinking, proactive game plan. On the contrary, if you're someone who doesn't care for career advancement and making more money, then a strategy or roadmap isn't needed. In fact, you can probably skip this chapter. But if you're someone who seeks to advance and eventually get to the top, keep reading because the path to the top can be a bumpy one if you don't have your ducks in order.

When thinking about career advancement, it's important to start with the foundational question of what type of employee do you want to be? There are two types of employees that exist at every company. There can be hundreds, thousands, or even tens of thousands of employees at a company, but each employee will fit into one of two groups: individual contributor (IC) or manager. An IC is an employee who contributes individual work and does not manage anyone.

Most employees at every company will fit into this category. Most junior-level employees, associates, assistants, and analysts are considered ICs. Even most software engineers are ICs. On the other hand, a manager is simply someone who manages people. This group typically includes directors, managers and senior managers, VPs, senior VPs, C-Suite executives, and other types of managers. Each group has its pros and cons that you should understand before you choose a career path.

ICs are the workhorses of every company. Companies can't function and grow without their ICs. It's like going to a McDonald's without someone making your order or hopping on a subway train without a conductor. Granted, many of these roles may be automated in the future, but that's a discussion for chapter 15. ICs have no management responsibilities. The core focus of an IC is to contribute individual work to the company's main priorities. There's a good chance that you, reader, are an IC. We all have to experience being an IC before we move on to become managers. We have to learn to do the work before we guide people on doing the work.

The upside to being an IC isn't so much what you get to do, but more about what you don't have to do. Managing people isn't easy. Most managers are bad managers because they don't understand people, how teams work, and how teams thrive. As an IC, you don't have to worry about team dynamics, leading and inspiring teams, managing, coaching, guiding direct reports, and all the other tasks that managers have to do. You can just focus on your work and the work of others around you and get paid. Sounds easy, right? However, the downside of staying on the IC path is the limited growth opportunities.

The folks who make it to the top have to become leaders. Most companies set up career growth paths specifically to create managers and leaders, not nurture ICs into becoming better ICs. After all, you can't become a director, VP, or CEO without having management experience. Because companies focus on that specific type of career advancement, employees who want to remain ICs throughout their careers don't have many options for growth.

Is it ever possible to grow while remaining an IC? It certainly is. At many companies, you'll find senior-level ICs who have climbed through the ranks. These are mainly subject-matter experts who have spent years honing their craft and making a difference with their expertise. Some of these ICs may have titles that include the terms strategist, principal, expert, advisor, or evangelist.

Most senior-level ICs may have never had the desire to become managers of people. Although corporate structures favor management, managing people is not for everyone. That doesn't mean that ICs will never have opportunities to lead. Leadership skills can be exhibited in different ways.

For example, you could be a leader of a project. In the tech industry, product managers are people who oversee the development, testing, and deployment of software and hardware. They lead teams of engineers and designers to create engaging software and hardware products that people want to use. But, in many cases, product managers don't directly manage people. They don't have direct reports, and they're not responsible for the career growth of their teams. They simply act as project leaders, but they're no less of a leader than actual people managers.

Becoming a manager is a whole different ball game. Managers are the strategic leaders of every organization. They set strategy, set priorities, set guidelines and rules, build teams, and inspire. Managers are the bosses. These are people who hire and fire. These are the people who make the big bucks but also have the biggest responsibilities. Managers are highly coveted in organizations because it's not easy being a manager. Not only do managers have to have a pulse on their teams, but they also have to make sure that their teams are successful and are able to work efficiently and hit goals. And when none of this happens, managers bear the responsibility. They're the ones who have the tough meetings with executives and board members. They're the ones who feel the pressure when employees aren't satisfied. They're the ones who have to make the grim decision of firing laggards and laying off people because of budget cuts.

The good thing about becoming a manager is that the path has most likely already been set for you. Companies value managers, so they create career paths to groom new managers. All you have to do is show off your leadership abilities and make an impact on the company, and you'll be well on your way to the top. Managers also get paid well, and if you're a top-level manager at a Fortune 500 company, you'll get paid really well. Almost too well.

Executive compensation is off the charts. For example, according to the Economic Policy Institute, the average pay of CEOs at the top 350 firms in 2018 was $17.2 million![3] By no means is taking the manager path a guarantee to that level of compensation in your career, but if you become an effective manager at a company with big coffers or a high-performing company, you'll definitely earn more than any IC would ever earn.

But with great power comes great responsibility, and managers have a lot of it. One of the downsides to pursuing the manager path is the pressure and stress. There's no doubt that most managers become more stressed than ICs throughout their careers. This is because managers bear the responsibility of their team's performance. As an IC, your performance is a reflection of you. On the contrary, as a manager, the performance of your team or department is a reflection of you. As a CEO, the performance of your company is a reflection of you. When things go wrong, it's your job to fix it. And if things don't get fixed, your job is in jeopardy. It's tough to constantly live with that sort of pressure, but that's why managers get the big bucks.

As a manager, you also have to take criticism and feedback well and turn it into positive action, which isn't easy to do. Feedback and criticism will come from everywhere—direct reports, other employees, other managers, the executive team, board of directors, investors, customers, partners, competitors. Managing the inflow of feedback and information and turning it into positive action seems impossible. Managing is not for the faint of heart or for those who want to shy away from the spotlight or the pressure. That in itself makes the managing path a route that many won't dare take.

I've contemplated taking both paths. For most of my career, I've had aspirations of becoming a chief marketing officer and leading a marketing department. But as my career progressed, I've become increasingly fond of the IC path. Being a manager isn't the most glamorous thing in the world. My first experience being a manager was one that I welcomed with open arms. I was eager to be someone's boss. The actual experience was duller than I expected it to be, but it was extremely rewarding.

In some ways, I can imagine being a manager is like being a parent (I have no experience being a parent). Your goal as a manager is to nurture and facilitate growth among your direct reports, remove barriers, and create an environment in which they can thrive. Your goal is to also set priorities and steer them in the right direction. If that doesn't sound like being a parent, then I guess I'll make a horrible parent and should stay far away from kids. However, the best part about being a manager is seeing your direct reports thrive because of your actions. There's nothing that says "I'm a good manager" like having a high-performing team whose needs are being met.

After figuring out whether you want to take the IC path or manager path, it's best to determine where is the best place to grow. Every company has different practices for facilitating employee growth. Companies tend to follow industry best practices, but I've found that some companies will tweak these best practices to their liking. When it comes to thinking about your growth at a company, hierarchy matters a lot. Most companies have a vertical hierarchy, which you're probably most familiar with. These are companies that have a top-to-bottom structure that makes it easy to visualize and understand where the growth opportunities lie.

For example, you know that as an associate marketing coordinator, you're several levels away from the chief marketing officer role. It's easy to grasp how long it might take you to get to that role in the future. On the other hand, some companies don't have much of a hierarchy. Instead, they have flat or horizontal organization structures. These are companies that don't have levels of managers and executives, but instead put an emphasis on functional leaders, squad leaders, and ICs.

The flat or horizontal organizational structure makes upward mobility difficult. Because there isn't a revolving door of managers and there aren't many levels of seniority, getting promotions becomes difficult. You can't really get promoted if there's nowhere to promote you to. Of course, a company can arbitrarily give you a more prestigious job title, but it may not mean much in reality. Flat organizations value ICs and leaders who aren't fixated on moving up. These types of structures exist to stamp out the bad traits of a vertical organization. Vertical organizations can become slow and political. Managers have managers who have managers who have managers. There may be several levels of managers in a vertical organization, which makes communication and efficiency increasingly harder.

Flat organizations value cross-team collaboration and team autonomy, and you may enjoy more work fulfillment working for a flat company. The downside is that the path for promotions and growth is more obscure.

Vertical organizations will give you more opportunities to grow and get promoted. The downside is that the way vertical organizations operate may not be efficient or best for the work culture. When making a decision about where you want to work, always inquire about the structure of the organization. This will help you determine how much autonomy you'll have, how much collaboration there may be, and how much growth potential there is.

Assuming that you're in an organization that has created guidelines for giving raises and promotions, you'll need to create a game plan for how you'll take advantage. Career growth is more than just getting raises and promotions, but raises and promotions will enable you to take on bigger challenges within your company and get paid accordingly. Asking for raises and promotions is more of an art than a science. Many career experts will lead you to believe that if you follow a set of best practices, you'll get what you want, but that's far from the truth. The reality is not only do you have to master the best practices, but you also have to know how to use leverage and perfect the art of timing.

In the first three years of my career, I never experienced getting a raise or a promotion. I simply didn't stay at the companies long enough to consider asking. However, my first raise and promotion happened in a better way than I expected it to. A little over a year into my tenure at my third company, I was kicking ass, to put it bluntly. I had followed the six-month rule and carved out a reputation for getting things done and working fast. I made sure in my first year to make my successes known so no one would doubt my impact. During my first year, I unexpectedly stepped into a leadership role in my team. My manager gave birth to her first child and went on maternity leave for three months. That left me as the most senior person on our team of three. There was a VP above me who led several teams, but he had a more hands-off approach, which made me the de facto day-to-day leader of our team.

That summer, I was eager for a raise. I made it my goal to make $100,000 per year by the time I was 30, and I was earning $75,000 at the age of 26. A nice raise would put me closer to my goal. For some reason, I was more fixated on a raise than a formal promotion. I had already taken on more responsibilities and didn't see a need for a job title change. But I wanted a higher salary to justify taking on more responsibilities and as an acknowledgment of my achievements. This was my first time asking for a raise, and I wanted to make sure I was prepared.

I scoured the internet looking for best practices on how to ask for a raise. I didn't lack confidence, but I wanted to make sure my method was bulletproof. Most experts suggest that you gather quantitative data on your achievements, so I spent a week putting together a presentation of everything I accomplished up until that point and made sure to include quantitative data to make the accomplishments more intriguing. I then sent the presentation to my VP with a request to meet to discuss a raise. I also made sure to set a reminder to follow up two weeks later if I heard nothing back.

About five weeks after I shared my presentation, my VP set up a last-minute meeting with me, the topic being unknown. Now, I'm not an anxious person, but whenever someone wants to "talk" unexpectedly, it makes my heart pound. I'm not someone who likes surprises. I like to see what's coming to me. The meeting took place in a common area of a WeWork building (our office space at the time), and the topic was a raise and a promotion. My salary was being increased to $89,000 up from $75,000. That's an 18 percent increase, which isn't very common nowadays. I was also being promoted to senior marketing manager, a title that made me feel older than I actually was, but nevertheless felt like I deserved because of my accomplishments and leadership. This was my first time asking for a raise, and not only did I succeed, but I also got more than what I asked for.

What did I do right? Before even considering asking for a raise or promotion, you have to have the work to back up your ask. Many people ask for a higher salary or promotion without having accomplished much. Not only will it be a little embarrassing when you get rejected, but it can also be demoralizing and prevent you from asking again in the future. A good rule of thumb is to wait at least a year before asking for raises or promotions.

My request for a raise came almost exactly a year after my start date. A year gives you time to accumulate successes and for your manager to get to know you and the way you work. Raises and promotions are given not only based on what you've accomplished but also your potential. Your manager needs time to learn what your potential is as a leader. Four business quarters (one year) is more than enough time, and if you follow the six-month rule, your impact and potential will be as clear as day.

The next ingredient to successfully asking for a raise or promotion is data. As a mobile marketer, I made sure to include any positive data points related to increasing user engagement and retention in my presentation. Most companies like to believe that they are data-driven, which means any financial decision has to be supported by data. This means giving people raises and promotions has to be supported by data points. A company wouldn't want to give a low-performer a raise.

Your job is to make your accomplishments compelling through data, whether qualitative or quantitative. For example, saying that you surpassed your sales goal by 35 percent is way more intriguing than just saying you surpassed your sales goal. Or saying that you drove $1.5 million in revenue is way more intriguing than saying you increased revenue. Data equals proof. With convincing data, you can build a solid case for a raise or promotion.

The last ingredient is the timing. Many companies have cycles throughout the year when they give raises and promotions to employees. Your request for a raise or promotion will most likely be granted during one of these cycles. Off-cycle raises and promotions only happen in special circumstances. For example, if someone gets laid off or leaves the company. Spend the majority of the year building the case for a raise or promotion and continue to have performance and feedback conversations with your manager. Show that you're improving and building your accomplishments. Then, when a promotion cycle comes up, make your best pitch with supporting data.

There are also times when asking for a raise or promotion just doesn't make sense. Some companies go through periods of growth stagnation or financial difficulty, either due to economic factors or company performance factors. In this case, it's best to hold off on your request for a raise or promotion. Not only will it most likely be rejected, but you may also come off as selfish if others around you are being laid off and the company is struggling overall.

Ride out the storm while still staying motivated and making an impact. When things get better, make your request. If the storm doesn't end, and you feel like you're overdue for a raise or promotion, open yourself up to a new opportunity at another company. There's value in commitment, but your first commitment is to yourself and your well-being. Companies will take care of themselves. You have to do the same.

Growing within a company is not as clear-cut as it should be. Sometimes luck and politics determine whether or not someone has the upper hand in moving up the ladder. And we also know that demographics play a big part as well. For a long time, women and people of color have had a harder time moving up the ladder than white males.

No matter who you are, you have to have a game plan. And if you're a woman or a person of color, your game plan has to be bulletproof. Never stay complacent, and always look for the next best opportunity. When the time comes for your company to give raises and promotions, don't be afraid to be the first in line. A closed mouth never gets fed.

CHAPTER 6: THE TRANSITION

I don't think I've ever met anyone in my life who enjoys job hunting. It's a necessary evil, but it really sucks! Doing it several times throughout the first decade of your career sucks even more. You'll most likely find yourself job hunting a handful of times early on in your career. Some jobs won't pan out as you expected them to, some jobs you will outgrow, and some jobs will simply not be interesting anymore. Whatever the reason, you have to be prepared to go back on the job hunt. But this time it will be different because now you'll be someone with experience.

I've successfully switched jobs three times as of the writing of this book. Each job hunt was unique in its own way. There's one job hunt that I went through right before joining my third company that I consider to be my most transformational job hunt to date. My second company was considered a B2B (business-to-business) company whose primary customers were marketers. From the time I studied marketing in college, I had always wanted to work with everyday consumers at a B2C (business-to-consumer) company. My career path up to that point didn't align with my early aspirations, and I thought to myself that if I was going to follow my aspirations, I had better do it sooner rather than later. It's more challenging to switch industries and verticals when you're older. The best time to pivot and change your mind is during your early years. For this reason, after a year and three months at my second company, I decided to go back on the job hunt.

I've started every job hunt while I still had a job. This is something you should always do if you have the chance. Quitting a job with no clear path to another job can put you in a tough spot financially. If you have the financial cushion and you hate your current job, by all means, quit and enjoy your sabbatical. But if you're like most people, plan to navigate your job hunt while still in your current role. I spent weeks taking phone interviews with recruiters in small conference rooms in my office. It certainly felt uncomfortable, but I didn't have many options. I would schedule fake doctor's and dentist's appointments to go to interviews across the city. One day, I even took a phone interview in an old-school phone booth at the New York Public Library.

The cell service was abysmal, and I kept getting disconnected from the recruiter.

About a month into my second job hunt, I was at the final stages of the interview process with an online platform for selling and buying high-priced art. I loved art and thought the role was a great fit. The recruiter asked for two of my references, which indicated to me that I had the role locked. There's a 95 percent chance that when a recruiter asks for your references, barring any last-minute surprises, you'll most likely get an offer. But sometimes that 5 percent kicks in, and things go haywire. That's what happened this time around.

I got a call from the recruiter at 9 a.m. on a weekday. She told me that while they wanted to offer me the role, their new head of marketing decided to put the role on hold. This was the second time that something that seemed within reach was snatched away from me. Was I shocked? Not one bit. After my TripAdvisor debacle a few years earlier, I knew the job hunt was anything but smooth sailing, but it still sucked. However, I didn't let that deter me, and I wasn't desperate. I already had a job that could hold me over. I could take my time.

Two months after the change-of-heart call with the art-tech recruiter, I embarked on a long interview process with a reputable company. You may have heard of them. They go by the letters I-B-M. IBM is a mammoth of a company, and they've been around for what seems like forever (since 1911). IBM has over 350,000 employees, and 70 percent of their workforce is located outside the United States.[4] IBM is a B2B company that predominantly sells software to other businesses. This didn't align with my goal of working for a B2C company, but I didn't care. IBM was a big enough name to look good on my résumé, and I was excited for the opportunity.

What I didn't know about IBM is how rigorous their interview process is. Since they're a large company, they have layers upon layers of managers for every division and vertical. Over the course of my interview process, I had phone interviews with five different people, all at five different times! Each person was the boss of the previous person, and the whole division was distributed across the United States. I didn't have one single in-person interview. The interview process was complete madness.

The good news is every interview felt repetitive, so I gave each person the same answers as I gave the last person. It didn't seem like they talked to each other. Eventually, I had a last phone interview with the head honcho of the division, who was based in Georgia. She was very personable, and we had a great conversation. After the series of interviews, I was confident that I would get an offer. I had great conversations with each person. After going through that grueling interview process, I sadly didn't get the job. It all felt like a waste of time. Four months into my job hunt, I still didn't have a new job.

Over the next several weeks, I had phone interviews with all sorts of companies. I had an in-person interview at Hearst, which is a big magazine publisher with a shiny blue skyscraper in New York City. I had a phone interview with PepsiCo for a role on a newly-formed e-commerce team. However, nothing seemed to stick. I eventually went against my advice, and I left my second company. I wanted to take some time off to reset my brain and work on personal projects. Being unemployed for the first time in three and a half years felt weird but also liberating. I was unemployed by choice, and I had enough money in the bank to help me survive for five months without a job. I embraced my short sabbatical by brushing up on my coding skills and building my own website. Three weeks into my unemployment, I entered the interview process with two companies, one of which would end up being my next employer.

I had a good interview process with Foursquare. The location company, which was an early tech darling of the mobile app era, needed a content creator to help boost the visibility of their apps. I knew I was the man for the job. After I left the interview at their SoHo office in New York City, I was confident they would want me. Plus, they were a B2C company, which aligned with my career plan. While waiting to hear back from Foursquare, I never stopped applying for other jobs. I eventually stumbled upon a fin-tech startup called Stash that seemed intriguing. I scoured LinkedIn to look for the recruiter so

I could email them my pitch. Once I found the recruiter, I knew I was destined to work at this company. The recruiter had my last name.

I always look for ways to spice up my email pitches to recruiters, and this was a great opportunity. My last name is not common, and I don't meet many non-family members with my last name, so this moment was special. I reached out to the recruiter with a witty email about our common last name. She immediately got back to me, and we scheduled a phone interview for the next day. Directly after the phone interview, she invited me to an in-person interview. I was a little taken aback by the speed at which she moved, but I welcomed it, nevertheless. Right before my in-person interview with Stash, Foursquare's recruiter got back to me. They wanted to make an offer. I was conflicted. Do I take Foursquare's offer and turn down Stash's interview invite? Or do I go through with the interview and negotiate? It was opportunistic for me to do the latter.

During my in-person interview with Stash, I felt at home. It was a scrappy startup with lofty goals, and that was exactly my vibe at the time. It also felt extremely diverse. Every person that interviewed me was a woman, even though the company was run by two male co-founders. During my last conversation with my long-lost family member, who was the VP of People Operations, I told her that I received an offer from Foursquare and that if they were going to make a decision, they had better do it soon. Preferably within three days. I also requested that the job title be changed. The role was for a marketing coordinator, but I felt that I was a little too experienced for such a junior-level title. I wanted to be a marketing manager. The VP of People Operations agreed to bring me in the next day to speak to the CMO, which would be the final in-person interview. The next day after that, the VP of People Operations called me and gave me a verbal offer.

In the span of four days, I went from having one offer from Foursquare to accepting a better offer from a different company. I got everything that I asked for from Stash. An expedited interview process (with no reference request!) and a title upgrade. Plus, the salary was $10,000 higher than Foursquare's offer. I sent Foursquare what would be my first reverse rejection email. Instead of me getting the rejection email, I was the one telling the recruiter that I didn't want them anymore. It felt good, although I hate rejecting people in general. Five months after the start of my job hunt, I had a new role with a better title, higher pay, and most importantly, at a consumer-focused company. My career had been thrust into new heights, and I never looked back.

CHAPTER 7: THE HUNT PART II

When job hunting throughout your career, there are several components that you just have to get right. I like to compare it to a NASCAR race. Before a driver even races, the car itself has to have new tires, a running engine, working brakes, adequate shocks and springs, and a litany of other important parts before it can compete on the racetrack. When you're job hunting, you're in the driver's seat, and everything you've learned and accomplished up until that point is equivalent to the car you're driving. The most important component of your car is your experience.

Job hunting with professional experience requires a different strategy than job hunting straight out of school. There comes a point in your career when your education and degree don't matter as much as they used to. That point is approximately three years into your career. That's not to say that education doesn't matter at all. Recruiters and hiring managers are human, which means they possess unconscious biases. Having a reputable alma mater on your résumé will automatically give you a leg up on the competition, even if recruiters and hiring managers deny it. However, good recruiters and hiring managers can look beyond status symbols, and what matters most to them is your experience and your impact. Also, your degree may be extremely important if you're in a field that requires a specialized degree (e.g., medical professionals and lawyers).

When job hunting for the first time, your main goal is to sell your potential. Because you most likely don't have any professional experience under your belt, there isn't much to show potential employers in terms of professional accomplishments. You're simply trying to sell them on future accomplishments and elements of your personality and work ethic. When you go on the job hunt with professional experience under your belt, your goal is to sell your accomplishments and translate those past accomplishments into future accomplishments.

As someone with experience, employers expect to be able to see themselves on the receiving end of the gains you've made in the past for previous employers. For example, if you were a crucial player in driving sales for a past employer, your future employer wants to see you replicate and expand that success at their company. It's no longer a matter of what your potential is but rather what concrete items you can contribute as soon as possible. That expectation doesn't exist for a new grad.

To make yourself an appealing candidate to any employer, first create a story around your accomplishments. Start with the foundation of outlining the quantitative and qualitative achievements you've made. Create a document that you update with each of your accomplishments as soon as they happen. That way, when you're ready to look for a new opportunity, it'll be easy to dig into your archive of accomplishments and experience to see which one fits the best with the opportunity that you seek. Then proceed to create a narrative to hook future employers.

Your narrative is equivalent to your elevator or sales pitch. It's the one thing that people should know about your experience if they don't have time to read through every line item on your résumé or LinkedIn. Your narrative gives your experience life and personality. Most of your competition for a job will resort to letting their résumé bullets speak for themselves. This is the status quo. If you want to go beyond what your competitors do, you have to brand yourself.

For example, I've spent most of my career up until this point using creative marketing strategies to help the companies I've worked for achieve success. I have my list of qualitative and quantitative accomplishments, but what I communicate on my social media profiles, speaker bios, personal website, and any email pitch to recruiters is something that's more high-level and sexier. Here's my "brand statement" that I've run with for years: *Marketer and creator based in New York City who uses creative and strategic thinking to grow brands. I've helped companies grow with stellar, data-driven marketing, amazing content experiences, and creative strategies that generate near-immediate results. I'm a creative and technical marketer who has a strong penchant for people-first marketing, outside-the-box thinking, fast iterations, and bringing ideas to fruition.*

This may seem like a paragraph full of jargon, but when you read it, it creates an image in your brain of what kind of professional I am. And that image is what I want every future employer to have in their mind the moment they contact me. Let's dissect it. *Marketer and creator based in New York City who uses creative and strategic thinking to grow brands.* This sentence seems like a simple statement of who I am and what I do, but it does something far more powerful than just answering the question "Who are you?" It reframes my occupation into something that every employer wants: results ("*to grow brands*"). It also teases the method in which I provide those results ("*creative and strategic thinking*").

I've helped companies grow with stellar, data-driven marketing, amazing content experiences, and creative strategies that generate near-immediate results. This sentence goes into a little more detail into the "how" of how I grow brands. It's still high-level, but it provides more concrete examples. I also entice the reader with a time-focused phrase: "*generate near-immediate results.*" As I mentioned before, as someone with experience, employers want to be able to envision what you can do for them and how fast you can do it. Communicating that I've driven near-immediate results creates an expectation that I can drive fast results, which is always welcomed.

I'm a creative and technical marketer who has a strong penchant for people-first marketing, outside-the-box thinking, fast iterations, and bringing ideas to fruition. Lastly, this sentence goes into a little more detail about who I am and how I do what I do. This communicates that I'm someone who values customers, creativity, speed, and execution.

As a whole, this brand statement that I've crafted for myself creates a narrative for who I am, what I do, and the impact I can make. I don't leave it up for interpretation. I define it immediately. That way, any future employer will know who they're reaching out to and who's walking through the door for an interview. Your brand statement doesn't have to be as poetic and finessed as the example, but it does have to make it clear to employers what you're all about, and it has to be a statement of the culmination of everything you've achieved.

But, of course, job hunting is more than just creating personal brand statements. If a personal brand statement was enough to get a job, I think I'd already be the CEO of Nike. Unfortunately, there's more to the job hunt as an experienced professional. One of the more painstaking and gut-wrenching parts of job hunting is interviewing. Mastering the interview process is the next step once you've gathered your accomplishments and perfected your brand statement. Interviews are a necessary evil for job hunting. Employers need to get to know you, and there's no way to do that based on your résumé and cover letter. Despite wishful thinking, the interview will never be eradicated so long as there are jobs that have to be done by humans.

First, let's consider how interview processes are structured. Most companies follow a basic interview process that involves a phone screening and one or more in-person interviews. The phone screening is essentially a bullshit filter. Recruiters set up these calls to determine if you are who you say you are and if you're worthy of bringing in for in-person interviews. Your résumé gets you noticed, and the phone screening gets you in the door. Once you've passed the phone screening, your candidacy is handed off to hiring managers. A recruiter's job is to bring in the best candidates, but a hiring manager's job is to make the hiring decision and ensure that you're a good fit for the role and the team. It's your ultimate goal to impress the hiring manager, not suck up to the recruiter. The recruiter is the means to the end.

In-person interviews vary by company. Some companies will put you through a panel interview with multiple people and some companies will have you sit down with multiple people one-by-one. Some companies stick to basic questions about your experience and personality, some companies create a discussion around a take-home project, and some companies will want you to solve problems on-site (most common among engineers). There are many ways you can shake-up an interview process, but regardless of what the interview process is, your strategy should remain consistent. Perform with confidence, speak with thought, and show humility.

The number one factor that kills candidates is a lack of confidence. Being unsure about yourself and your accomplishments automatically puts you at a disadvantage and leads to displays of nervousness and uncertainty. Most hiring managers and recruiters are forgiving and understand that not everyone has ice in their veins. Some people get flustered in high-pressure situations, and that's okay. However, to give yourself the best chance of getting the role, make it a priority to suppress your nervousness and befuddlement. Think about why you're there in the first place. You're at the interview because someone likes you, they like what you've done, and they think it's worth their time to talk to you. That in itself should be enough to help you feel confident. Once you're at the interview, you're 50 percent of the way to your goal, and you've outlasted hundreds if not thousands of other candidates. That's a big reason to feel proud and confident.

Sometimes the feeling of nervousness doesn't come from a lack of confidence but instead comes from the fear of failure and rejection. Some people are afraid that despite all the hard work they put in to get an interview, they'll be turned down. Maybe they're desperate for a job and have a burning desire to leave their current role. Maybe they really need money and need to get a job as soon as possible. Whatever the case, sometimes fear of failure fogs your thinking and causes you to get flustered and screw up at the wrong time. This is the perfect time to embrace failure.

In chapter 2, I discussed overcoming rejection. You'll experience more rejection in the job hunt than in any other part of your life (unless dating is your favorite thing to do). In order to become better at interviewing, you have to suppress the forces that sway your composure. You can do this by reframing failure and rejection. At this point, you should see rejection as just a pothole in the road. If you have the right tires, the pothole won't crash your car, and you'll ride away largely unscathed. Rejection in the job hunt becomes the building block to success. Each time you're rejected, you have an opportunity to learn from what happened and fix your mistakes. Once you finally achieve your goal, it'll just be a culmination of all your rejections. Sometimes rejection happens even when you've done nothing wrong. Sometimes luck isn't on your side, and that's okay. In this case, you're only experiencing a slight delay in achieving your goal.

While in the interview, it's also important to speak with thought and humility. Above all else, hiring managers want to know how you think, how you solve problems, and how you can fit with the team. Quite often, interviewees will rush through their answers or try to recite some canned answers that they've memorized. This is a huge mistake. Don't view your interview as an audition. It's not a performance where you have to become something or someone that you're not. The interview is the time to have a discussion with a future employer. This discussion is centered around solving key pain points for the company or plugging holes that the company has. During this discussion, your main task is to demonstrate your ability to think critically, solve problems, and be open, honest, and genuine. You'll have to think quickly, but you do have time to think. Don't feel that you have to rush your answers or have a perfect answer to every question. After all, you are human.

Eventually, interviewing will become second nature. It'll be like washing your hands or tying your shoes. Over time, those interview butterflies won't be as prominent, and your confidence will grow. In any one job hunt, you may go through several interview processes, all differing in structure, length, and content. It's a test of your perseverance. You have to know going into any interview processes that there's a good chance you won't be chosen. But you also have to be confident that you will be chosen. And when you are chosen, that's when the fun begins.

When a company chooses to hire you, your work isn't done. Now you're at the offer management and salary negotiation phase, which can be as easy as Tic Tac Toe or as difficult as a game of chess. Every employer you encounter has already set aside a budget for the role you've applied for. Sometimes that target salary or wage is based on an industry average or standard, and sometimes it's based on what they can afford. Regardless of what they want, it's your job to know what you want, know what you're open to, and be realistic about what you can get.

First, do your homework on what a typical salary for the role would be. Try to adjust that number based on geography, years of experience, and industry. There are many online tools that allow you to pinpoint what an average salary looks like for the role. But going into any salary negotiation, your goal is to get more than the average. You want the most you can get. Some companies that pride themselves on providing competitive compensation will offer you more than the average, in which case your decision will be pretty easy. However, other companies may stick to the average or even lowball you. Here's your game plan.

Let's say your salary at your current job is $75,000. In a perfect world, you want to make anywhere between $90,000 and $100,000. You're also comfortable with making as little as $80,000, and the average salary for the role you've applied for is $82,000. When negotiating your salary, aim for your ideal range of $90,000+. If a company is uncomfortable with your counteroffer, they'll most likely encourage you to go down a little. But even if you tell them that you would accept, say, $85,000, that's still within your comfort range and well above what you currently make. When a company sees that you're willing to go down from your asking price, that'll show them you're a team player and willing to sacrifice to join the company.

However, keep in mind that this strategy only works if a company is willing to negotiate. Some companies will give you a take-it-or-leave-it offer, in which case you have to decide what you can live with and what your deal-breaker is. When considering an offer, never unwillingly compromise your quality of life and standard of living, unless that's what you choose to do. The last thing you want is to be in a situation where you're struggling to live. You may also find a company that's willing to offer you other perks and compensation besides the base salary (e.g., bonuses, stock options, etc.). Make sure to weigh everything carefully. Remember, you're making a decision about your livelihood. Despite the temptation to accept any offer, you have to weigh your options and decide what's best for your life, not what's most economical for the company.

If you're really lucky like I was in my second job hunt, you may have offers from different companies at the same time. This is the best position to be in. You can now pit companies against each other and reward the highest bidder if you like all companies equally. In my situation, which I described in the last chapter, Stash offered me a higher salary and a better job title than Foursquare, even though Foursquare's offer was the first one. Foursquare had more brand recognition, but their offer was $10,000 below Stash's offer. Plus, helping people invest and grow their money was more meaningful to me than helping people find the nearest ramen spot. My decision was easier than I thought it would be, but it may not be the same for you.

When considering different offers, first decide on which company you would prefer to join. That's the company that you'll be willing to negotiate with a little more. With the others, use your leverage and be a little greedy. Show them that other companies want you, and if they want to hire you, they need to increase their offer. Be aware of each company's comfort zone. Most companies aren't willing to go above what they've budgeted by too much. Once you know each company's limit, you can weigh your options appropriately and make a decision. None of this is relevant if you get the right offer from your dream company. If that happens, take it. Don't wait. But most of us don't get offers from our dream companies, and we have to use a little leverage and creativity to get the right offers from the less desirable companies.

The job-hunting experience is different for every single one of us. Some people seem to get a job with the snap of a finger, and others struggle endlessly to find a company that will hire them. There are many factors that can affect our chances of success, and those factors vary as well. What's most important is that you have a strategy for getting what you want and knowing how to replicate that strategy when it works. However, having a strategy doesn't mean you won't struggle. The job hunt will be tough, and sometimes you need a little luck on your side. But with perseverance, grit, and a thoughtful blueprint, you'll be luckier than the rest. I promise you that.

CHAPTER 8: WHAT'S YOUR BRAND?

Think about your favorite brands for a second. Who are they? What do they offer? How do they make you feel? What do they represent? My favorite brand of all-time is Nike, and almost everyone I know knows this about me. As I mentioned in chapter 1, sports was a major part of my childhood. Everything that I wanted to be as an athlete, Nike stood for. Owning anything with a Nike swoosh on it made me feel elite. I felt like I was a part of a global community of athletes who bled and breathed sports. There are other global brands that make people feel the same way. For instance, many customers of Rolex watches or other Swiss luxury brands have come to trust the quality and craftsmanship of Swiss products. Swiss brands exude an aura of excellence in craftsmanship, and many rich folks and luxury goods fans soak it all in.

Now take those same thoughts and apply them to people and public figures. Who are they? What do they stand for? How do they make you feel? Some names may immediately pop into your head. For me, some of those people go by the names of Martin Luther King, Jr. and Barack Obama, just to name a few. These are people who, aside from their historical and societal impact, have unique personas and personalities. These are people we can identify just by reading a quote, hearing a trivia question, or reading a piece of their writing. We can identify these people with little effort because we know what they stand for and what they represent. They have something that all of us have the capacity to build: a personal brand.

A personal brand is how you present yourself to the world. Your personal brand encompasses what you do, what you represent, and what you value. More importantly, it's the public perception of what you do, what you represent, and what you value. It's commonly accepted that a personal brand is developed in an intentional and conscious way. In other words, it's something that you actually put in the effort to develop over time. However, I argue that a personal brand is also something that you've built subconsciously and unintentionally.

I doubt that Martin Luther King, Jr. thought of his personal brand when he spoke out about the various injustices of American society, and I highly doubt that Barack Obama thought of his personal brand when he decided to run for president to provide hope to millions of underrepresented Americans. Yet, they've unintentionally and subconsciously built public personas that many admire, by merely being men who wanted to make a difference. Their personal brand is what we remember most about them. When we think of these two men, we can think of the words that they represent: hope, justice, equality, progress. In Barack Obama's case, his personal brand has allowed him to help others outside of the presidency through the Obama Foundation and other philanthropic initiatives.

Your subconscious personal brand is not something that you can consciously develop. Your subconscious personal brand is made up of your personality, your behavior, your personal values and goals, and your personal experiences. Your subconscious personal brand is something that develops naturally. However, your subconscious personal brand can take a back seat to your conscious personal brand. Your conscious personal brand is the personal brand that you want everyone to see. It's the personal brand that you intentionally build, curate, and refine over time. It's the personal brand that you'll use to get ahead in your career.

Admittedly, the concept of a personal brand can seem silly. After all, we're human and imperfect. We're not objects or corporate entities that need labeling, branding, or categorization. In a perfect world, I would completely agree with this. No one should feel the need to control or curate how others perceive them. In a perfect world, we would all just be our unapologetic selves, with our dark flaws and all. But, sadly, this is not a perfect world. And specifically, in the professional arena where perception and reputation matter a ton for career growth, you need to be smart with how you're perceived.

Building a personal brand gives you two main advantages: (1) it shows the professional world that you exist, and (2) it helps you build an authoritative presence if you so choose to. Before I go deeper into these two advantages, I want to emphasize that a personal brand is not required for career growth and success. Millions of professionals around the world are able to build successful careers with little to no personal branding. Believe it or not, most people still don't have a personal website. Personal branding is merely a propellant, but it's a strong propellant that can work wonders for your career and accelerate your career success, faster than that of your peers.

The first advantage of personal branding is that of making your existence known. What this means is that you want people in your industry and domain to know who you are and what you do. This is a basic level of personal branding. By doing as little as buying a domain for your name (e.g., donteledbetter.com) and setting up a website and LinkedIn account, you're taking claim in ownership of your name. Now, whenever you apply for jobs or look to capitalize on any other opportunity, people will know who you are within a few clicks. In an age where searching Google is more common than brushing one's teeth, providing others with the luxury of an instant, basic profile of yourself is smart.

Without this first advantage, it's like you're swimming underwater. No one would know who you are, and the only time people would hear from you is when you apply for a job. When recruiters consider candidates for roles, one of the first things they do is search the person on the internet. This is not specifically an effort to dig up dirt; it's an effort to get to know you before they actually have to spend time getting to know you. It's an effort to size you up and prejudge you.

Not only do recruiters do this, event organizers, investors, potential mentees, and any other party that can give you an opportunity do this as well. Your best bet is to make it easy for them by showing what you want people to know about you. This helps clear up obscurity about your identity and helps people see you through your point of view, not theirs. You never want someone to create your narrative for you. It's your job to lead the way to make sure you're seen in a favorable light.

The second advantage of personal branding is what will elevate your personal brand and open doors for your career. This is the effort to become an authority or expert. Let me warn you that this is a path that you should tread carefully and strategically. In this day and age, there are many self-proclaimed thought leaders, experts, and gurus who do more self-promotion and monetization than actually providing guidance, thought leadership, and expertise. In reality, your authority or expertise will be largely determined by others, not by your own self. It's up to your audience to determine whether or not your content is helpful and best-in-class.

Experts and thought leaders are people we look to for guidance. Anyone can have wisdom and relay guidance, such as your parents, but what makes an expert different is the size of their audience. Most industry experts are known throughout the industry. If you're practicing to become a great chef, you might look to chef Gordon Ramsay for tips and advice. If you want to improve as a stock investor, you might look to Warren Buffet for guidance on investing. However, thought leadership is not only reserved for celebrities and public figures. Anyone can be an expert and thought leader in their own industry or domain, even on a small scale.

The first component of becoming an expert is experience. When you're seen as an expert, there's an assumption among your audience that you have experience and success in what you're preaching. Without this basic requirement, no one will consider you an expert, and you shouldn't consider yourself one either. Experience and success are generally built over the course of years, which means your expertise may not be recognized until much later in your career.

Even with a long time horizon, you should always take stock of your career success and share your thoughts, strategies, and opinions with others. This can be done through social media, guest blogging, your own blog, and other mediums. When you get into the habit of sharing strategies, tips, and opinions on relevant topics in your industry, you build a treasure chest of information that can be immediately useful to your peers.

Of course, your treasure chest of opinions, tips, and strategies is worthless without an audience. Every expert starts out with an audience of one—themselves. Building an audience takes hard work and patience, but the caveat here is that having a massive audience is not required to become an expert. Yes, there are many experts and thought leaders who have massive followings on social media, hundreds of thousands of monthly visitors to their website, and big email lists. But these are exceptions to the rule. In fact, many experts are people who provide their expertise behind the scenes and tap into the audiences of other organizations to spread their wisdom.

In college, I had a few professors who had done great things in their careers. My statistics professor in my junior year spent 30 years working for companies like IBM and Boeing. I had another professor who was a well-known scholar on race relations in America. These weren't modern-day thought leaders by any means. They didn't have massive online followings or highly successful websites, and to this day, they probably still don't. However, they're still able to provide their expertise through various publications, academic journals, and reputable organizations. They don't need an audience because they can piggyback off the audience of a larger entity to get the word out.

When you become an authority, you become someone that others want to hear from. The more you share your experience and provide your thoughts and expertise in your domain, the more you build your credibility and status as an authority. This automatically raises your public profile and creates demand for your time. One of the most exhilarating positions to be in, in your career, is to have a stream of opportunities flowing your way with very little effort. It's a position that most people don't have the privilege to be in, primarily because they haven't put themselves out there.

When I started my career in content marketing, I used blogging as a way to provide opinions on hot topics in the industry as well as share successes to inspire others. As I established myself as a practitioner in the industry, I slowly gained more credibility and eyeballs. Eventually, I became someone others wanted to hear from and work with. As a result, I gained more opportunities to speak at events and conferences, to be a guest writer on various blogs and websites, to mentor, to consult and freelance, and to work full-time at different companies. Today, I've become accustomed to getting inbound interest from recruiters about job opportunities. It's a position that I don't take for granted and am extremely grateful to be in.

But it's also a position that I know I've earned because of how I've been able to establish myself as an expert.

Personal branding with a foundation of authoritative thoughts, ideas, opinions, and success will bring you an immense amount of opportunities to grow your career. It's not something that's required for career growth, but when you have it, and it works, it's like having a cheat code to success. That is, of course, if you like the spotlight. The light shines brighter from the brightest stars.

CHAPTER 9: BUILDING A NETWORK

The first networking event I ever attended was during my freshman year of college. The event was on a Sunday, and I had skipped partying with friends the previous night to wake up early and make sure I looked presentable. I wore baggy dress pants and a shirt that was a size too big. The purpose of the event was to meet people in the industry and potentially discuss internship opportunities. At that point in my life, I wasn't good at small talk. All I knew was how to hand out my résumé. I didn't understand the point of networking and didn't think I needed a "network." I thought the concept was stupid, and to this day, I think the concept of networking needs to be redefined.

Your network is your web of connections. These connections are coworkers, former coworkers, partners, clients, mentors, former classmates, former professors, and other people with whom you've established a relationship. If you're wondering, yes, your friends and family are indeed a part of your network. Almost every piece of career advice related to networking suggests you should compartmentalize the people you know into personal and professional connections. While this makes sense in most aspects of your life, when it comes to your career, don't make that distinction. You can create more opportunities for yourself and vice versa by expanding your perception of who's helpful to your career and who's not.

Your network serves as your support system throughout your career. While friends and family are the only ones who can really support you personally, there's a larger nucleus of loose connections that can help you thrive in your career. They can provide things such as career advice, job opportunities, partnership opportunities, mentorship, new areas of learning, new customers, and more. These are people who may know either your strengths, ambitions, passions, work ethic, accomplishments, personality, or all of the above. They're the ones who can write letters of recommendations, invite you to exclusive events, introduce you to cool people, give you insider tips, and endorse you for job openings.

Of course, despite what it seems, it's not all about you. Any healthy relationship needs to be mutually beneficial and reciprocal. Your network doesn't exist only for your benefit. To nurture the relationships within your network, you have to be a provider as well. This means being someone who's willing to help when called upon and even proactively thinking about others when you come across relevant opportunities. For example, if you have a connection who's looking for a new job, and you spot a job opportunity that the connection is perfect for, don't hesitate to reach out and make them aware. This is just one example, but there are many of these moments that you can't be too selfish to pass up. Be willing to pay it forward.

Back during my first job, I was responsible for hiring freelance writers to help us write online content. Nowadays, hiring freelancers can be such an impersonal task. Some freelancers you may never even see or talk to in person, video chat, or on the phone. Communication is typically done via email or a chat platform like Slack. This was the case with one freelancer I hired. Her name was Heather, and she had her own business writing content for various companies. She wrote several pieces of content for us, and over time, she became my go-to person when I needed help writing (remember, I was a one-man show).

Fast forward several months, and I found myself looking for freelance writing opportunities. I was looking to supplement my job income with a short-term freelance gig. During that time, Heather had built up her business into a well-known company for helping sales teams write cold emails. She was pretty good at delivering and perfecting her service, but she needed help. Luckily, we stayed in touch after I left my first job, and she was able to reach out to me and offer me freelance work helping her write cold emails for clients.

That freelance work helped me earn a few thousand dollars and improved my cold emailing skills, which I still use to this day to reach out to recruiters and basically anybody else I want to get in contact with. Despite the fact that it's been six years as of the writing of this book since we did freelance work for each other, we've still remained in touch. In fact, we've met up on several occasions, both in San Francisco and New York. She's invited me to a birthday house party that she held, and I've taken her to my favorite speak-easy cocktail bar in New York City. I've reached out to her for advice on entrepreneurship, and she shares my writings sometimes.

Am I best friends with Heather? No. Do we meet regularly? No. We've met up less than ten times in the past six years. We're nothing more than casual friends that can benefit from each other in different ways professionally. She's as much a part of my network as I am a part of hers. And whenever there's an opportunity or idea that reminds me of her, that'll be a reason to reach out and nurture the relationship. Luckily, that's easy to do nowadays. Digital communication eradicates your excuses for not reaching out. A person is only an email, text, or social media message away. My relationship with Heather is a golden example of how a professional connection can turn into a personal one and be mutually beneficial.

The "what" and the "why" of building a network are crystal clear. But the "how" is more obscure and leads many young professionals to a dead end. It's important to realize that some people may not be naturally equipped to create and maintain loose connections that make up their network. Some of us are more introverted and tend to shy away from interactions. Up until midway through my college career, I wasn't someone who was very interested in getting to know people who didn't have something I wanted. I'm an introvert from birth and always valued having a handful of close friends and family rather than a web of loose relationships with random people. But as I progressed in my career, two things happened: I became more socially active and my network expanded exponentially.

In the beginning of my career, I saw networking as a task—something I had to do to get ahead. I attended a countless number of networking events, only to collect a stack of random business cards from people I had no intention of ever talking to. I hated any event that was predicated on the notion of "networking," but I especially hated connecting with people with no real purpose. However, as I started benefiting from the networking concept (e.g., my connection with Heather), my perception changed. Not only did I understand why it was important to connect with people, but I also became more enthusiastic about looking for opportunities to connect.

Networking quickly evolved into something more natural. It became a habit. No longer did I dread reaching out to people from the past, going to events and meeting strangers, and requesting to stay connected to people I met. This activity became something that I felt I should always do any chance that I got. As with most things that I've mentioned in this book, it became a mindset. This mindset helped me build a web of connections that have enriched my life and career.

When building your network, condition yourself to avoid thinking of it as a task. Once it becomes a to-do list item, it'll be something that you feel sucks away your time and energy, and you'll try to avoid it every chance you get. Instead, view it as you would view your daily commute to work. In a perfect world, you would never have to commute to work (world events in 2020 are making this a reality). But in a non-perfect world, your commute is necessary for getting to your place of work. It becomes a routine that's automatic, even though you'd prefer not to do it in your perfect world. Networking is the same way, although, in a perfect world, you still may want to keep in touch with certain people that you meet because they enhance your life.

Furthermore, networking is not just the process of going to events and meeting strangers. Even today, I despise networking events for networking's sake. They always seem dry and weird, and I always run into people who just want to make a sale. I generally stick to events where there's actual content to be consumed and networking is merely a perk, like a conference. This allows me to put my time to good use even if there's no one around that piques my interest enough to talk to. Networking events are held to essentially encourage people to meet others, but they always come off as forced. Instead of sticking to RSVPing to formal networking events, take a more proactive approach and network with everyone you meet, even the bus driver or local hairstylist.

The perfect group to build a network off of are coworkers. Think about it, these are people you interact with every single day, in some cases more than you interact with family and friends. The workplace is a great environment to get to know, learn from, and help others. And when it's all said and done and you or your coworkers leave your company, you'll still have the shared experience of working together. Having the shared title of being an alumnus automatically makes people want to help you when you need help. That shared identity of being an alumnus of a company or school creates an invisible bond that you can use to your advantage if you're smart.

Of course, there are other 21st century ways of connecting. With platforms like LinkedIn, Twitter, and Instagram, you no longer have to meet people in person to connect with them. If there's someone you're interested in talking to, you can just reach out to them.

However, always proceed with caution when doing this. Unsolicited messages and requests can turn people off. They're equivalent to knocking on a random person's door to strike up a conversation. This won't go over well with most people, but if you have an interesting reason why you want to connect with someone or if you both have interacted via online social gestures like sharing, liking, commenting, and retweeting, then don't be afraid to shoot your shot.

On LinkedIn specifically, there's this practice of "open networking" that frankly needs to be flushed down the toilet. Open networkers are people who connect with people on LinkedIn for the purposes of being connected on LinkedIn. They have no real purpose as to why they want to connect with you, and many of them are focused on increasing their connection counts to look popular. Believe it or not, that is still a thing nowadays. Followers and connections are like currency to many people. I beg you to not become one of these open networkers.

There's a difference between having loose connections and being virtually connected to people you've never talked to or met a day in your life. Loose connections serve a purpose and have a reciprocal benefit. These are people you've met or talked to at some point in time and have established that you want to remain in touch for some benefit or no benefit other than being friends. They're not close friends, but they're also not complete strangers. There's a baseline familiarity and commonality that you share with these connections.

Connecting with random strangers virtually makes "connecting" meaningless. It takes seconds to "connect" with someone on a digital platform, and most requests to connect are either for some superficial benefit such as connection counts or self-serving benefits such as more eyeballs on a person's content or more sales. That's not to say that purely digital connections can't turn into something more. There are many stories of people who have met clients, friends, partners, mentors, and even spouses through digital platforms that aren't explicitly dating platforms. But for every decent connection you make online, there are ten others who just want to use their connection with you for some self-serving reason.

In regard to career growth, they say it's not about what you know but who you know. I've heard this phrase so much in my career that I hate hearing it. But, unfortunately, it couldn't be truer. In today's corporate environment, having a web of people who can support you, vouch for you, hire you, and teach you is more valuable than what you think you know about getting ahead. This web of people automatically gives you an advantage that many people don't have.

That advantage is a flock of enablers. These are people who want to see you succeed, who like you, and don't mind lending you a hand. For a good part of my life, I thought I could succeed without the help of others. I thought I could put on my Superman cape and do it alone. To say I was wrong would be an understatement.

CHAPTER 10: THE MOMENTS THAT TAKE YOUR BREATH AWAY

Most of us grew up with a really dark vision of work. We've envisioned slaving away at some job that we hate just for a paycheck. We've envisioned bad bosses, annoying coworkers, and coming home grumpy every single day. Unfortunately, this vision is a reality for a lot of us, but it may not always be. You may find a role in your career that you really enjoy. A role that brings you genuine joy. A role where you meet great people who become friends. A role where you end up dancing next to your CEO at a nightclub in Las Vegas on a weekday. Yeah, about Vegas. I have a story.

When I started my role at my first company, I wasn't the only one who joined the company at the time. I joined the company alongside another guy who was studying to get his master's degree at NYU. He hailed from India and attended undergrad at UC Berkley in California. Although we came from different backgrounds and we were two years apart in age, we had similar stories and we were both in the same boat. We were two young professionals who came from poverty. We were both joining a tiny startup with a very small chance of long-term success. We hit it off pretty quickly and established a routine of having lunch together, eating at fancy restaurants after work, and discussing life.

Then ten months later, we embarked on a trip to Las Vegas with our CEO (who was our manager). A large part of our customer base was a group of marketers called affiliate marketers, who make money selling products from other companies. These marketers are scrappy and always hungry for tips and tricks to make a profit in online and mobile advertising. Every year, multiple times a year in multiple locations, this group of marketers congregate for a conference called Affiliate Summit. Affiliate Summit is the premier conference for affiliate marketers, and the yearly destination for the west coast version of the conference is Las Vegas. In January 2015, my new work buddy and manager/CEO traveled to Las Vegas for Affiliate

Summit West to meet our customers and nurture our customer relationships and party.

If you would've told me in college that my first work trip would be to Las Vegas, I would've laughed. No one goes to Vegas to "work." Absolutely no one. So, it was no surprise that this "work trip" to Affiliate Summit West was riddled with cocktails, affiliate marketing dudes with lots of money, affiliate marketing dudes who wished they had money, and scantily clad women. Yes, we did meet customers there as well as other vendors and potential customers. But at the end of the day, everyone at the conference, who were mostly men, came to Vegas to party.

A few nights into our time there, we found ourselves at Hakkasan, which is a popular nightclub in Vegas right beside the MGM Grand Hotel. We hit the dance floor right alongside our CEO, which is the most awkward thing you can ever experience. Not to say our CEO wasn't cool, but he's not supposed to be cool. He's supposed to be a superior. At least, that's what they tell you in school. Long story short, that work trip ended in us meeting a handful of customers, and me having my first party experience in Las Vegas.

I believe good moments can happen at work, and work can bestow upon you unintended positive experiences. My Vegas story is only one of a few great, fun, and weird work moments I've had in my career. And my friendship with my coworker was the first, but it certainly wasn't the last. In my career, I've had the privilege of experiencing some of the most amazing moments, such as being accepted to a startup accelerator by Disney and Techstars and subsequently flying out to Burbank to visit Disney's campus. I've flown to San Francisco to help run a conference and modeled for an advertising campaign at my second company. I've been on a few cruises for milestone celebrations at my third company. And I've spent five weeks in Finland getting to know my European coworkers at my fourth company.

When you go through your career, keep your eyes open for experiences and people that can enrich your life. It's easy to see work as something solely transactional. You do the job, you go home, you get paid, rinse, and repeat. But there will most likely be opportunities to establish friendships, travel, meet industry experts and public figures, and find new passions. Obviously, if work is a place where you don't want to be, then it'll be hard to see the value in doing more than the bare minimum. But if you enjoy your job and the company that employs you, stay involved in your company's culture and become someone who raises their hand.

Work culture and benefits nowadays are specifically designed to keep you engaged as an employee. Some say it's a way for employers to keep you working longer. I partially agree with this notion. But I think the desire to retain employees and drive increased productivity is stronger than the desire to simply keep them working longer hours. Modern-day work cultures introduce benefits such as team outings, education stipends, daily or weekly lunches or breakfasts, demo days, happy hours, holiday parties, milestone celebrations, and other various activities. Why do employers spend so much money on these seemingly wasteful activities? Because they work in increasing employee morale.

As an employee who may be showered with these sorts of perks throughout your career, it's only your moral duty to take advantage of these to enrich your life. These perks didn't exist for our parents and grandparents. Work was never a place to have fun for them; it was a way to survive. Now, the tables have turned, and work can become a destination for personal enhancement, growth, and dare I say, entertainment.

Furthermore, is there any value of having work friends besides the obvious benefit of being able to gossip and complain to someone? Well, of course, there is. Work friends give you a support system. Things can be hard at work. There are many things that can drain you at work, including challenging tasks and projects and annoying coworkers or bosses. You need a sounding board and go-to destination for managing these situations. That destination is ideally someone who can understand your situation based on a shared experience. If you need action to be taken, that warrants a discussion with your manager or someone in management. However, there are times when you need someone to talk to, not necessarily to take action. That's when work friends come in. Work friends are your family when you're working. They're a valuable support system for your time at work.

Having work friends can also benefit you outside of your immediate workplace. Work friendships are like any other relationships in that if you put in the work, they can last a very long time and be mutually beneficial. One way these friendships can be mutually beneficial is for referrals and recommendations. There will come a time when you will have to separate from your work friends and find a new job at a new company. Life will diverge, and you will no longer sit next to the one person you've seen every single day for the past three years. That doesn't mean your relationship should stop.

When the time comes to apply for new roles, apply for grad school, or do any other activity that requires others to vouch for you, you can reach out to your work friends to make that happen. To be clear, it's important to also keep in touch when you don't need a favor. You can damage the connection that you have with someone by always having your hand out. But work friends are unique in that they know how you work. They have a front-row seat to your work ethic, your successes and failures, your work style, and personality. These are insights that even your spouse may not see on a day-to-day basis.

Overall, work is what you make of it. If work to you is just a means to get a paycheck, there's nothing particularly wrong with that. There's more to life than just work. But if you want to enrich your life through work, then you have to open yourself up to new people and new experiences at work, even if that means going outside of your comfort zone. When life gives you lemons, make lemon meringue pie.

CHAPTER 11: BEING AN OUTSIDER

The feeling of being a Black person in the tech industry is a lonely feeling. Almost everywhere I look, no one looks like me. I've attended a countless number of meetings in my career where I was the only Black person in the room as well as the only person of color. I've been a part of teams where I was the only person of color. I've been to professional events where I was the only Black person in the room.

I've become accustomed to feeling like an outsider. It's so second nature to me that sometimes I'm not even aware of the lack of diversity in tech. If you're someone who's part of a minority group—whether that's racial, ethnic, gender, religious, or disability—you may find yourself the only one of your kind in certain situations. I have good news for you. Being an outsider doesn't have to feel like the worst thing in the world, and it doesn't have to hinder your career. You can turn it into a weapon for good—a weapon for change. As an outsider in a minority group, you're already making an impact that you may not even know about: you're setting an example.

When I joined Stash, I was one of a handful of Black people at the company. You could literally count on one hand how many Black people there were at the company. Most companies don't share metrics on employee diversity publicly, so as a candidate who wants to join a company, your only source of information are the reviews on a website called Glassdoor or the images that companies feature on the careers page of their websites. At the time, Stash featured several employees on the careers page, and I was included in that group. It turns out that what I thought was a fairly meaningless photo of myself with a white sweater holding a DSLR camera turned out to be a source of motivation for several other Black people who joined the company months after I did.

About two years after joining the company, I found myself having lunch with a group of ten Black coworkers at the company. The number of Black employees increased significantly during my time there, which I completely credit to the HR department of the company. Now, you couldn't count the number of Black people at the company with one hand; you needed about three! Well, certainly two. During that lunch, it felt amazing to be around people who looked like me. All of us were from different departments and teams—some were engineers, some were in operations, some were in legal and compliance. To me, this was a snapshot of how tech companies should look.

Throughout our various conversations, one engineer said something that I didn't expect. He told the table that one of the main reasons he applied for his role was because he saw my photo on the careers page. Several others around the table also said the same thing. My photo was a source of motivation. These revelations made me proud, a little emotional, but also added a little pressure. I realized that I was unknowingly someone's inspiration. I was able to set an example by simply being at the company. And not only being at the company but being in a mid-level role at a young age and being a constant voice in important conversations around the company related to key projects.

Setting an example as a member of a minority group doesn't have to happen consciously. This can be considered a passive action. Passive action is an effort that doesn't really seem like an effort. It's not something that you actively have to do. Being someone's role model or inspiration isn't an action that you're taking in a literal sense, but it's an action that you're creating with either your mere presence or your normal day-to-day behaviors.

By being the best you can be and breaking barriers, you may be a source of motivation for hundreds of people who want to be in your shoes and want the opportunities that you have. That's the power of being an outsider. Your presence as an outsider inspires others like you, and this is a power that you should always know that you have. But you can take it a step further as well with something called assertive action.

Assertive action is our proactive effort to make a change. Companies are stubborn in that they don't want to change what they already think is working. If an all-male, all-white executive team is able to drive year-over-year revenue growth, why change how the executive team looks? Things are working just fine as is. As an outsider, it won't be easy to be a driver of change, especially if you're someone who isn't outspoken. Being a driver of change means taking some risks and sticking your neck out for causes bigger than yourself. The causes can range in scale and magnitude, and some causes you won't be able to lead on your own.

Within the workplace, there will be many causes and issues you will feel obligated to speak out on. They won't all be related to issues of race, gender, ethnicity, or any other hot, button-pressing societal issue. For example, you may feel that your team is overloaded with work. Or you may feel like your team is never a part of important meetings and discussions that affect customers. Whatever it is, these issues provide an opportunity for you to speak out as an outsider; someone whose opinion or belief may not be shared with everyone else around the company. What it takes to get your voice heard as an outsider is a set of supporting data and internal sponsors.

Data is the bedrock of any decision-making process. Companies like to believe that every decision within the company is based on some qualitative or quantitative data. This means that any case you want to make for changing any aspect within your company has to have supporting data. For instance, if you want to make the case that your team's perspective isn't being heard in relation to important customer issues, it may be worth running a survey to collect qualitative feedback from the rest of your team to back up your claim. If the overall sentiment of the survey answers suggests that the team feels left out of important conversations, then you have sound data to back up your case and present it to your manager and any other stakeholders.

Then, you'll need internal sponsors. These are people in your organization who will support your case and provide any supplemental data, anecdotes, and evidence. These may be fellow outsiders whose contrarian beliefs coincide with yours. The reason you need these people is because collective efforts are more powerful than individual efforts, and if you're an employee who doesn't have the power to make unilateral decisions, you need to build support to make a change.

Toward the tail end of my time at my first company, there was some tension at the company. None of it can be considered serious, but there were communication gaps about the performance of our company, which obviously affected the work I was doing. Since the company was small (there were only seven people), there was a small likelihood that I would find someone who felt the same way I felt. This in itself was intimidating. Bringing up an issue alone would've made me look like the boy who cried wolf or would've made my case weaker.

Luckily, I was able to discuss the issue with my now good friend who I joined the company with. Together, we had a meeting with our CEO and discussed the lack of communication in the company, specifically around company performance. Having a co-sponsor on this topic helped boost the severity of the issue, and ultimately led our CEO to make a significant effort to improve communication.

Several years later, I found myself in a similar situation. This time, the company was bigger (100 employees), and the number of co-sponsors on the topic at hand was seven. A big upgrade from one person! The topic this time around was pretty similar to the aforementioned issue. Our team felt that there wasn't enough communication about the impact we were making, and the communication that was happening wasn't dictated by us. Others around the company had wrong, preconceived notions of what we were doing as a team. There was also the issue of feeling like we were the punching bags of the company. Collectively, we made our voices heard to our VP. Without this collective effort, nothing would have changed. Fortunately, over time, we saw that things started to change. Processes were tweaked to ensure that our team's impact was noticed, and that's all we wanted.

It's quite common to feel powerless in an organization. After all, we're just building out someone else's dream, right? At least that's what wanna-be entrepreneurs always tell you. But I'm here to tell you that you have power as an outsider. As someone who has to break down barriers and bulldoze the foundation of the status quo, your power is present within convincing data and collective voices.

Companies make changes when the forces supporting change outweigh the forces against change. Your role as an outsider is to either spark that change or join other outsiders to drive that change, or both. Change doesn't come easy, but it's almost always worth the blood, sweat, and tears.

CHAPTER 12: WORK-LIFE DICHOTOMY

The average person will spend 90,000 hours in their lifetime working.[5] That's approximately a third of your life spent laboring away for a paycheck and some benefits. I don't know about you, but that statistic makes me a little depressed.

Ask anyone what their purpose in life is and very few people, if any, will say "work." For almost all human beings, work is a means to an end. If we all had a choice, we wouldn't be working in the traditional sense. Life requires some degree of work (e.g., gardening), but in terms of doing tasks that you don't personally enjoy or benefit from as a source of income, that's something that most of us would readily do away with if we could. But since we can't, we have to figure out a way to make work fit into our puzzle of life. We have to carefully establish our work-life balance.

Work-life balance is a state of equilibrium between your career and your personal life. Your personal life includes the things that you love and enjoy, like family, friends, your free time, and hobbies and interests. Many people tend to compartmentalize work and life. Work is seen as something that's not complementary, and instead, it's an interruption to what really matters to a person. However, the issue with this thinking is that it sets an expectation that you'll never be truly satisfied as long as you're a working person. What you need to do is flip this notion on its head and instead focus on making work and life comparable to the point where there is no work-life balance; it's all just life.

The way to do this is to first change your approach of how you view work. One of the most popular pieces of career advice that's constantly pushed on young professionals is to do what you love, which makes sense in theory. If you love pets, it only makes sense to work with pets at an organization like the ASPCA. The issue with this advice, however, is that it lacks some practicality and may limit your career growth.

The saying goes, if we all did what we loved, we would never have to work a day in our lives. But in many cases, what you love isn't well-monetized and is devoid of career opportunities. For example, my personal passion is photography. I would love to get paid as much as I do as a marketer to take pictures. However, photography is a very competitive space with very limited earning potential in the long-term. Sure, I can try to start my own photography business, but starting a business is always less secure than having a salaried job. The effort that's required to make photography work as a viable career with growth opportunity just isn't worth it.

If your passion happens to fall within a space that's growing and has broad career opportunities, then you're in luck. However, if you're like most people, whose personal passions don't translate well into thriving careers, then you need to lean on something else. You need to focus on doing what you can tolerate and what you're good at. This is a very pragmatic way of thinking, but I did warn you that this is an honest guide, not an optimistic and hopeful thinkpiece.

Focusing on what you can tolerate and what you're good at opens up many more opportunities for career exploration. Your passion directs you to one door, but your skills and tolerance give you many doors to walk through. Let's say, for example, you've proven to be a really good project manager. You're someone who's organized and is able to flawlessly help companies push projects and campaigns to completion. With that skill in mind, you can look for companies that you wouldn't mind working for. Ideally, these are companies that have products or services that you believe in. Instead of looking for the perfect company and perfect role that aligns with your passion, you're looking for a company that has a great offering that you admire and that needs your professional skills.

This is the first part of making work better and more comparable to your life. You're not looking for the perfect fit with limited opportunities, you're looking for the right fit with endless opportunities. That gives you more freedom and possibilities. The second part of making work better and more comparable to your life is finding a company that actually values employee well-being and the right to balance. A company that values employee well-being and the right to balance is a company that prioritizes the physical, mental, and emotional health of its employees as well as creates policies and processes to allow employees to unplug from the demands of work.

I've worked for startup companies throughout my career where the work environments are hectic around the clock. I've spent late nights in the office and at home working. I've had to shift around weekend plans to work. I've received work calls, emails, and messages while on vacation. I've received work calls, emails, and messages while partying. I've lived the quintessential startup life where work never stops and hustle culture is prominent. It's a lifestyle that most startups don't want to let go of for fear of not being productive or scrappy. But it's a lifestyle that I realized I didn't enjoy all that much.

Although startups are known for this type of work culture, this can also exist in larger companies. It depends on the industry you're working in, the company's leadership, and your specific role. For example, companies on Wall Street are known for having burnt-out employees. There are hundreds of stories of financial analysts staying at the office until midnight to wrap up reports. The same goes for marketing and ad agencies. Far too often, work bleeds heavily into a person's personal life, and the balance is thrown out.

The balance is also uneven when you're part of management or an executive team. Managers and executives have more work demands than lower-level employees, and in many cases, there's an expectation that they are "always-on," even during nights and weekends. The further you move up a company's ladder, the more work will bleed into your personal life. In some ways, it's the price you pay for having more responsibilities, a higher salary, and a more powerful role.

The way to find out if a company values employee well-being and the right to balance is to speak to current and former employees. What you're looking to learn are honest assessments of the work culture. You want to know how often they have to work on the weekends and at nights, how often are they contacted by managers and executives about seemingly urgent matters, and how well does the company provide opportunities for employees to unplug, take breaks, and work on all aspects of their health. But even if you do your due diligence and get the inside scoop of what life is like at a company, you still may never know until you experience it yourself. There are risks in joining any company, and one of those risks is joining a company that's secretly running a figurative sweatshop where employees are depressed, unhappy, and burnt-out.

When it comes to the balance of work and your personal life, it's more your job than your company's job to make sure that the balance stays even. You have to create personal standards and guidelines for yourself that'll help keep work from being a detrimental part of your life. For example, after my years of working for startups and feeling like I was on-call every waking minute of my life, I set guidelines for myself on how I will manage work communication. I am adamant about not communicating about work on the weekends and vacations unless there's an emergency. Of course, this will change as I move into more powerful roles, but it's a luxury I plan on keeping for as long as possible.

I am also extremely conscious of my workload. Early in my career, I had no barometer for how much work I was taking on. I was someone who volunteered for almost anything, and I didn't know how to say "no." Eventually, I became overwhelmed, and I would let some things slip through the cracks—something I'm not known for letting happen. Learning how to say "no" is important because we all have limited capacity. When we say "no," we learn how to prioritize what's important. Over time, I became good at declining to do things that weren't important to the company's goals or pushing them off for when I would have adequate time and headspace to work on them. This helped me improve my mental health and head home every night feeling empowered, not torn down.

Having a job that you're satisfied with at a company that prioritizes employee well-being is the foundation for viewing work as a complementary component of your life. There's no doubt that if you hate your job, you'll never view work as a positive aspect of your life. We avoid the things we hate. So, focus on finding a role that, ideally, you enjoy and can tolerate. It doesn't have to be the role that aligns with your passion. But it does have to be a role that allows you to live your life and be happy.

CHAPTER 13: FINDING YOURSELF

I thought I knew myself. I thought almost thirty years was enough time to learn who I am, how I like to work, what my pet peeves are, what types of teams I like to be a part of, what types of companies I like, and what type of manager I could tolerate. But one thing that you'll learn as you progress in your career is that what you like and how you like to work is slowly revealed over time. It's like spending years putting together a puzzle, and the puzzle pieces are all the individual experiences that you've had.

Finding yourself when building your career can be a challenge. Taking time for self-reflection is an activity that far too many people seem to deprioritize. As a result, some of us feel lost in our jobs. We feel frustrated in our jobs because we don't know exactly what we want from our jobs, from our managers, and from our coworkers. We also feel conflicted about our feelings about our jobs. We experience so many feelings on any given day that when we finally have time to think about our jobs, we can't quite summarize our feelings. This is why finding yourself early in your career is essential to your career development.

"Finding yourself" means being self-aware and knowing who you are, what you like and dislike, what you value, and what triggers you. It's closely related to emotional intelligence, which has become a hot topic in the fields of self-help and professional development. Emotional intelligence is the capacity to control, express, and be aware of one's emotions. It also encompasses the ability to handle interpersonal relationships. I like to use the term "finding yourself" because it's less of a scientific method and more of an iterative personal process.

Online articles related to emotional intelligence will have you think that there's a blueprint or playbook for finally being emotionally intelligent as if it's an end state. The process of being intimate with your feelings, needs, and desires is a process that will never quite end. To help break this down, I'll use the two main pillars of emotional intelligence: self-awareness and self-management. While there are four main components of emotional intelligence, self-awareness and self-management are the ones most closely related to finding yourself.

Self-awareness is arguably the most important component of the process. This is your ability to understand your emotions in any given moment, how certain events affect your emotions, and the impact your emotions have on others. A simple demonstration of this is receiving critical feedback from a coworker about your work on a project. A lot of us will immediately feel defensive when we receive negative feedback because we feel attacked. Simply knowing how you feel in that moment and how it affects you is considered being self-aware.

The reason why I say that self-awareness is the most important component of emotional intelligence is because a lot of what you'll feel throughout your career will be driven by others, and it's important to know which events are triggering which emotions. Working with other people inherently creates a complex environment. Everyone has different personalities, motivations, degrees of power, and skills. You'll often find yourself in difficult situations with others that will evoke certain emotions. For example, feeling betrayed after a coworker takes credit for your work. Or feeling disappointed after you've been passed up for a promotion. Not being able to identify what you feel in any given situation can negatively impact your emotional health. A feeling that can't be identified is a silent threat to your emotional stability. Once you gain the ability to identify your emotions, the next step is learning how to manage them and your behavior in any given situation.

The second component of emotional intelligence is self-management. Self-management is your ability to control your emotions and behaviors, adapt to the changing environment around you, and respond to external events in healthy ways. The most quintessential example of bad self-management is losing your cool and blowing up at your boss. Maybe this is okay to do in movies and TV shows, but letting your emotions get the best of you, even in a bad situation, makes you look out of control and pushes you to do and say things that you end up apologizing for later on. You never want to be in a situation in your career where you have to apologize for your behavior. This is where self-management is important.

The key to improving your self-management skills is perfecting the time period between identifying the emotions you're feeling and the resulting actions. In my life, I've benefited greatly from being a person who thinks before I speak. Every action I take is a result of an assessment I've made in the seconds, minutes, hours, and days prior. In pressing situations where an immediate action or response seems easiest, you have to force yourself to think about the ideal way to act.

Let's use the example of a coworker taking credit for your work. A person with poor self-management would immediately get angry and lash out at the coworker, potentially damaging relationships, damaging their reputation, or maybe even being fired as a result. Unfortunately, these situations happen far too often because many people lack self-management or self-control. In this situation, a person with good self-management can acknowledge that they feel backstabbed and hurt.

What they can then do is take time—maybe a few hours or a day—to think about how to approach the coworker and talk about the situation. Maybe the coworker will eventually apologize and make things right. If not, you always have the option of talking to your manager, who might help you receive the recognition you deserve. The second option in this situation helps you preserve your reputation and can even boost it once people see that you know how to respond well in crappy situations.

Finding yourself in relation to your career is more than just perfecting emotional intelligence. Building a career that you can be proud of requires being mindful of all the things that make up a career. Everything from the type of company you like to work in, to the type of managers you like to have, and to the type of work cultures you thrive best in. This all needs to be contemplated on a regular basis as your needs and desires will most likely change. Not keeping tabs on how you feel about these things can leave you in a state of confusion and discontent about your career because what you want from your career can't actually be pinpointed.

I was always an independent person. At an early age, I had the mindset that I could stand on my own two feet without much guidance and could tackle any challenge on my own. When it came time to figure out my financial aid situation for college, I didn't have much help from family partially because I didn't ask for help. Since my parents didn't have money to send me to college, I felt the onus was on me to figure everything out. I took it upon myself to learn the ins and outs of taking out student loans, grants, and scholarships, and essentially put myself through college with minimal intervention. Throughout my late teenage years and early adulthood, I became accustomed to the feeling of autonomy. My maturity helped me thrive in this world of self-governance. However, what I did not know is that autonomy would be the most important thing for me when it came to work.

I realized early on in my career that I work best when I have autonomy. I don't do well with micromanagers. In my eyes, micromanagers have a lack of trust in their direct reports. I become frustrated and ultimately lose motivation when someone is hell-bent on trying to hold my hand and micromanage me. Knowing this about myself helps me avoid situations and opportunities where micromanaging is the norm. Every job opportunity that I pursue has to come with a prerequisite of autonomy or at least some degree of autonomy. I'm well-aware that complete autonomy is unrealistic in most cases, so when I pursue job opportunities, I make sure to ask questions about the areas in which I'll be able to have the most leeway in doing what I know how to do best.

Autonomy may not be the most pressing issue for you. It may be the opportunities to collaborate with others or opportunities to be recognized for your work. Whatever it is, make sure you're able to identify your needs and desires as you move along in your career. They'll surely change, but as long as you constantly reassess what your "deal-breakers" are, you'll be able to better search for and filter out job opportunities.

The emotional intelligence layer of finding yourself is a foundational layer that you should aim to work on early in your career. Emotionally intelligent employees are some of the most productive employees because they can maintain their composure and productivity in almost any situation. The second layer of finding yourself is knowing your needs and desires. Answering the questions "What do I want?" and "What do I need?" is essential to finding the right career path. Leaving these questions unanswered can lead you down a path of confusion and frustration. The third layer is a bit more obscure but equally important; it's knowing your purpose.

CHAPTER 14: WHAT'S YOUR PURPOSE?

I always think about what goes through the minds of people who work for companies that aren't doing much good for society. The example that pops into my mind constantly is tobacco companies.

By all measures, cigarettes are extremely harmful to human health. Almost no one disputes that, not even the tobacco companies themselves. However, the tobacco industry is still significant in our economy. People still smoke, and tobacco companies still make a profit. And there are thousands of people who make a living off of people smoking. This is not a book about ethics and morality, but that whole situation is pretty screwed up to me.

I'm one of those people who don't believe that humans have an actual purpose from birth. This is also not a book about religion and spirituality, so I won't get into that either. But the idea of having a purpose is relevant to careers. The organizations that we work for have a profound impact on society, whether positive or negative. When we think of organizations with a positive impact, we think of nonprofits like the Cancer Society or World Health Organization (WHO), or for-profit companies like Proctor & Gamble, which makes products that help us take care of ourselves (e.g., toothpaste and shampoo). When we think of organizations with a negative impact, we think of tobacco companies, companies that make guns, companies that build prisons, etcetera (of course, it's all relative).

As a professional, you have a choice to decide which companies you work for. Early in your career, you may be less inclined to think about the societal impact of the company that's writing your check. After all, if you have the same mindset that I had at the age of 22, you just need a job, and you don't care about who's giving it to you. However, as your career progresses, you'll have more choices, and you'll have to decide which of those choices closely align with your core values as a person.

During my second job hunt, when I was exploring a transition from a B2B company to a B2C company, my personal values helped me make my decision on which company I wanted to work for. My B2B experience was all about helping marketers from other companies better advertise and communicate to their customers. This was a cool problem to solve, but I felt emotionally detached from the issue. After all, I couldn't care less, personally, about the quality of other companies' marketing and advertising strategies. Normally, emotion doesn't matter in business, but I wanted to feel something about what I was doing. I wanted to feel proud and know that I was making an impact on millions of regular folks. I didn't feel that in B2B.

When it came down to choosing between working for Foursquare and working for Stash, two companies with consumer-focused apps, the decision was easy. At the time, Foursquare had a cool app that helped people find places around them, like shops and restaurants. This is something I saw myself working on, but when I compared Foursquare to Stash, Stash came out on top. They were building an app that helped people invest in the stock market.

This resonated deeply with me because I grew up below the poverty line. My family didn't have a lot of money and definitely wasn't great at saving and investing it. But, like my family, there are millions of Americans who don't understand the wealth-building advantages of the stock market and shy away from it either because of fear or simply because they don't have the resources to invest.

Stash's app not only gave people an accessible way to invest in the stock market through a concept called fractional shares, they also provided guidance and education around personal finance. Learning how to manage your money is one of the most underrated life skills, and unfortunately, it's not widely taught in schools at any level. I firmly believe that Americans—and especially people of color—need to learn how to manage their money to build their wealth. Stash's offering aligned perfectly with my beliefs, and I chose Stash over Foursquare.

Once I joined Stash, I made a personal promise to myself to always work for companies that have a net positive impact on humanity. This simply means that, at the end of the day, any company I work for has to be doing something positive for the world. This personal promise automatically disqualifies many companies. You'll probably never find me working for an alcohol brand any time soon. At this point in my career, I get a healthy amount of inbound interest from recruiters about various job opportunities. Before even considering the role, I always do research on what the company provides as a product or service. If the company doesn't satisfy my net-positive-impact-on-humanity rule, it's an automatic "no."

You have to find your career purpose. The reason is when you progress through your career, your view of work will change dramatically. As the world changes around you, and as you start to open your eyes to more global issues, you'll feel an increasing urge to do something about these issues. Or at least do something that doesn't torch the earth. You don't want to find yourself working for a company that's doing something that goes against your values and what you've established as your purpose. More importantly, you don't want to find yourself contributing to the decay of society.

So how do you do it? How do you find your career purpose? Just look at your personal values. Sit down and figure out what you believe in, how you hope to shape the world, what an ideal world looks like to you, and what elements of society you wish you could eradicate. There are thousands of companies solving all sorts of problems around the world, and there will surely be a few that would be a great fit for you. Also, look beyond the big problems. Obviously, the likes of climate change, racism, and poverty are some of the world's most pressing problems that need to be solved. But there are other issues and shortcomings that you can focus on.

For example, as of the writing of this book, I'm employed at a Finland-based company called Yousician. We help millions learn how to sing and play musical instruments, namely guitar, ukulele, piano, and bass. The lack of people playing music isn't a pressing global issue, but studies have shown that music improves mental health. Music is also an important aspect of world cultures. When I think of my personal promise and Yousician, the two are in perfect lockstep. Yousician has a net positive impact on humanity.

During the first decade of your career, you'll get the urge to address that burning question that we all ask ourselves: "What am I doing with my life?" For some people, this is a very literal question. They literally don't know what they're doing and have no plan. But for others, like me, this is a question that hides an even deeper question: "What impact do I want to make?"

To have an impact, you need to find your purpose. And your purpose lives within your personal values.

CHAPTER 15: 21ST CENTURY THINKING

As I mentioned in the first chapter, I wanted to be in the sports industry when I started college. Nothing about my ambitions suggested that I would be doing anything else other than doing something for a team in either one of the four major American sports leagues (NBA, NFL, MLB, NHL). But life had the final say, and I ended up in the tech industry, and specifically the NYC tech startup scene. To say I lucked out is an understatement.

The world is changing around us. Climate change is threatening our globe, which is leading more industries to innovate around green energy. Consumers don't want to own anything anymore (RIP CDs), which means creators are offering their creations on subscription-based services like Spotify. Consumers are providing more data to companies, which means companies have more tools to personalize experiences and more weapons to do harm. Most importantly, computers are getting smarter, which means, naturally, companies are finding new ways to cut costs and automate everything.

There are many forecasts for how big the artificial intelligence (AI) industry will be by the year 2030. I'll spare you the numbers, but let's just say it'll be big and exponentially bigger than it is today. AI is something most people can't quite comprehend today, even though it has gained popularity and there has been enormous progress in the past decade. AI gets all the news coverage, but it's not AI that regular folks like you and I need to worry about; it's automation.

Automation and AI are two fundamentally different things. Automation is completing tasks without human intervention. AI is a bigger field of applying intelligence to computers. The reason regular Johns and Janes like you and I need to worry about automation is because automation is happening right now. While true artificial intelligence is a long way off, automation is helping companies cut their employee headcount. If you've visited a fast-food restaurant like McDonald's recently, you've probably seen it in action. In most McDonald's around the world, you can order from a kiosk, which removes the need for a human taking orders.

What this means for regular folks is that your job may be at risk if it can easily be automated. Again, this is honesty talking. Companies can and will become more efficient at operations as they find new ways to automate. The costs for setting up a system for completing tasks is almost half as much as paying the wages or salaries of people. When building your career, you need to start thinking about the future and what technology means for your industry and career potential. For-profit companies won't stop implementing more automation to employ more people. For that reason, you need to be nimble.

When looking for job opportunities, do a deep assessment of the job opportunities that you're seeking. Are they roles that can be easily automated? Is there any data around the obsolescence of the role? Is the role currently in-demand or will it be in-demand in the future? Now is the time to start thinking two steps ahead. Yes, a career path may seem promising now, but in five years, that may not be the case. Take stock of the world around you and go down the career path that's evolving alongside the world, not being left in the dust.

Some of the most in-demand jobs as of 2020 exist in the technology field. Software engineers and data scientists are two of the most in-demand roles in all of tech, and they'll most likely continue to be in-demand for the next 10 years. According to indeed.com, as of August 2020, the average salary of a software engineer in the United States is $110,071. The average salary of a data scientist in the United States is $121,618.[6] Of course, these are only averages, and salaries span the spectrum. Also, these averages can be skewed by those engineers and data scientists who get paid the big bucks at companies like Google and Facebook.

Not only is the earning potential in tech relatively high, but the career opportunities are growing every day. Innovation around AI, automation, health technology, financial technology, and other industries is rampant. As someone who may not have the skills that are required to do the work of a software engineer or data scientist, you may be asking yourself how you can get involved in tech. There are two ways to do this: readjust or pivot.

The great thing about skills is that they're transferable. The skills you learn in one area can be applied to another area. This isn't as true for hard skills because the software you learn in one industry may be completely irrelevant in another. But soft skills, like organization, communication, emotional intelligence, and leadership will always remain relevant no matter where you go. If you're someone who wants to get into tech, you can focus on reapplying your skills to the needs of the tech industry.

For example, let's say you're a fifth-grade teacher, and one day you decide to get into the tech industry. You can use the teaching and communication skills you learned while teaching to help a tech company improve its customer support team. I once had a manager who was a teacher in a former life. She eventually became the director of product marketing for Stash years later. Who would've thunk it! Or, let's say you have excellent Excel and analytical skills that you've acquired doing book-keeping at a former role. You could become an analyst on a company's customer support or data team, assuming you're willing to learn additional software. Skills can always be reapplied, and they can be your gateway to the tech industry.

If reapplying your skills doesn't get you to the tech industry, you can also make a career pivot. As I mentioned in the first chapter, making a career pivot is easier early in your career. As a young professional, you're not as entrenched in your industry and you don't have years of experience in a specific domain under your belt. You also may not have personal obligations to hold you back (e.g., having a child). A career pivot to tech basically means learning new skills that'll directly apply to the tech industry.

In more specific terms, this means learning software development, data analysis, product management, IT, product design, or UX research. There may be more entry points to the tech industry, but those are the main options. You'll find many organizations that are willing to provide courses and certifications for those disciplines. Many universities also offer post-grad degrees and professional courses.

There are also non-tech-related roles that can get you into the tech industry. Every tech company needs business operations and marketing. For almost the past decade, I've been responsible for using various marketing strategies to help tech companies acquire and keep customers around. Although I've gained various technical skills since I started my career, my career didn't start out as a technical career, and I didn't have a technical education. Over time, I became a non-tech employee who understands technology and the way it works. That's helped me excel in all my roles and opened up opportunities for me to pivot to a more technical role if I chose to.

If you're someone who wants to get into tech, there are an abundance of ways to do it. All you have to have is the drive and desire. Those of us who have found ourselves in the tech industry in some capacity from the 1990s to today have benefited handsomely from everything tech has bestowed upon our society. Not only have companies like Apple, Google, Facebook, and other dominant tech startups disrupted our lives in unprecedented ways, but they've also given their employees a great source of income and, more importantly, keys to the future.

This chapter may seem like a plug for the tech industry, and it kind of is. However, it's more about the reality that tech will continue to dominate and transform our lives for years to come, and the opportunities will grow exponentially. Whether you like it or not, your career will be defined by what's happening in the tech industry. You may choose to pay attention, or you may choose to turn a blind eye to evolution. I implore you to do the former. But don't just pay attention—act. Be opportunistic and go where the opportunities exist. Think about the future, and be a few steps ahead of your peers who are still stuck in the present. The future's calling us, and it's our job to pick up.

Hopefully, I'll see you in the future. Hopefully, you'll be doing better in the future than you're doing right now. Hopefully, when the future gets here, you'll be prepared to weather any storm and tackle any challenge. And hopefully, you don't lose your mind along the way.

EPILOGUE

This book doesn't touch on every single thing anyone needs to know about building a career. Job hopping, public speaking, résumés and cover letters, and becoming a manager are just a few topics that deserve deep dives and critical analysis. However, the guidance in this book is what I believe to be the foundation for any young professional who wants to take control of their career.

Quite frankly, I was fed up with seeing some of my peers and friends lose hope when it came to finding the right job. We are trained to think that employers have all the power, and we're just living in their world. We subject ourselves to misery because we feel like we have no other alternatives or we're not good enough to get the job that we want. This is why there is such an obsession with entrepreneurship. Entrepreneurs don't have to put up with the nonsense and power dynamics regular people do. They run their own companies and can make their own decisions, and that apparently makes entrepreneurship a way better alternative to having a steady job.

My hope is that this book helps reveal the power that you already possess as someone with a regular office job. Your career is yours, so you have to take control of it in an unapologetic fashion. That means going after your goals by any means necessary and building a career that you deserve. When you feel beaten by rejection, discouraged to pursue your ambitions, or confused about where to go next, remember the principles that this book teaches you. Don't think too much about your next step—just take it. Don't think too much about your next interview—just do it. And don't think too much about creating the perfect career plan—just make it work.

BIBLIOGRAPHY

[1]Clance, P. R., & Imes, S. A. "The imposter phenomenon in high achieving women: Dynamics and therapeutic intervention." Psychotherapy: Theory, Research & Practice, 15(3), (1978): 241–247.

[2]Young, Valerie. The Secret Thoughts of Successful Women: Why Capable People Suffer From the Imposter Syndrome and How to Thrive in Spite of It. New York: Crown Publishing Group, 2011.

[3]Lawrence Mishel, Julia Wolfe, "CEO compensation has grown 940% since 1978," Economic Policy Institute, August 14, 2019, https://www.epi.org/publication/ceo-compensation-2018/.

[4]Vindu Goel, "IBM Now Has More Employees in India Than in the U.S.," New York Times, September 28, 2017, https://www.nytimes.com/2017/09/28/technology/ibm-india.html.

[5]Pryce-Jones, Jessica. Happiness at Work: Maximizing Your Psychological Capital for Success. Wiley-Blackwell, 2010.

[6]Indeed.com, https://www.indeed.com/career/software-engineer/salaries.

ABOUT THE AUTHOR

Donté Ledbetter is a senior marketer who has spent years working for fast-growth startup companies in the tech industry. He is on the list of "20 Black Leaders To Follow For Career Inspiration" by FindSpark. He has spoken to audiences at New York University, Montclair State University, State University of New York at New Paltz, and various marketing conferences. He has also written for Elite Daily, Advertising Week, and VentureBeat.

Made in the USA
Monee, IL
04 November 2026

67387326R10085